Emotional Intelligence 2.0

Mastering the Digital Era's Challenges by Navigating Emotional Burnout, Overcoming Distractions, and Thriving in Today's Complex World

Madison Harper

Table of Contents

Dear Reader,

Firstly, thank you. By picking up "Emotional Intelligence 2.0," you have embarked on a journey that I hope will enlighten, empower, and perhaps even transform the way you perceive emotions and human connections. But before we delve into the heart of the matter, I wanted to share some guidance on how to make the most of this reading experience.

Come with an Open Mind: Our emotions, behaviors, and beliefs are shaped by a myriad of experiences and teachings. As you read, you might come across ideas that challenge your existing perspectives. Welcome them. Reflect on them. Growth often starts with discomfort.

Pace Yourself: While it might be tempting to rush through and consume everything at once, I encourage you to take your time. Let each chapter simmer in your mind. Some concepts might resonate immediately, while others require deeper contemplation.

Apply as You Learn: Emotional intelligence, at its core, is experiential. It's not just about understanding, but about applying. Try out the strategies and techniques in your daily life. Observe the shifts in your interactions and inner dialogues.

Engage in Reflection: At the end of each chapter, pause for a moment. Think about how the content relates to your own life, and jot down any insights or personal anecdotes that spring to mind. This book can serve as both a guide and a journal of your emotional journey.

Share and Discuss: Emotional intelligence is, in many ways, about connecting with others. Talk about what you learn with friends, family, or colleagues. Share your challenges and triumphs. You'll be surprised at the rich discussions that can emerge from these conversations.

Revisit: Our understanding of emotions evolves as we do. What resonates with you now might take on a different hue in a year or even a month. Keep this book close, and revisit it whenever you feel the need.

Lastly, remember that while this book offers tools and insights, the true expert on your emotions is you. Trust in your journey, in the process, and most importantly, in yourself. Here's to a deeper understanding, richer relationships, and a more emotionally attuned you.

Warmly,

Madison Harper

Introduction

Emotional Intelligence, often abbreviated as EQ (Emotional Quotient), is the capacity to be aware of, control, and express one's emotions, and to handle interpersonal relationships judiciously and empathetically. Unlike traditional intelligence, or IQ (Intelligence Quotient), which focuses on cognitive abilities and logical reasoning, EQ centers on the heart of human experience – our emotions and how we navigate them in ourselves and in relation to others.

At its core, emotional intelligence challenges us to go beyond the surface of raw emotion. It asks us to delve deeper into understanding why we feel a certain way and how these feelings can influence our decisions, behaviors, and interactions. EQ provides a framework for recognizing the emotions of others, discerning between different feelings, and labeling them appropriately. It also equips individuals with the tools to use emotional information to guide thinking and behavior, and manage and/or adjust emotions to adapt to environments or achieve one's goals.

While the term itself might seem modern, the nuances of emotional intelligence have been a topic of philosophical and psychological discussion for centuries. From ancient Greek philosophers contemplating the nature of human emotion, to modern-day psychologists exploring the depths of human consciousness and interpersonal dynamics, the quest to understand our emotional world is both timeless and ever-evolving.

Understanding EQ is not merely an academic endeavor; it's a deeply personal one. Our emotions influence every aspect of our lives—from our closest relationships to our broader social interactions, from our most significant life decisions to our daily routines. By grasping the essence of emotional intelligence, we open the door to a richer, more fulfilling life, rooted in understanding, empathy, and authentic human connection.

The roots of emotional intelligence can be traced back to early human civilizations. Ancient philosophers, poets, and thinkers have long been intrigued by human emotions and their impact on behavior and decision-making. While they didn't use the term "emotional intelligence," their writings and musings often reflected a deep understanding of its principles.

In ancient Greece, philosophers like Socrates, Aristotle, and Plato pondered the nature of emotions and their role in rational thought. It was Aristotle who famously said, "Anyone can become angry – that is easy. But to be angry with the right person, to the right degree, at the right time, for the right purpose, and in the right way – that is not easy." His words resonate with the modern understanding of EQ – recognizing and managing emotions in a way that is both appropriate and beneficial.

Jumping ahead to the 20th century, the formal study of emotional intelligence began to take shape. In the 1930s and 1940s, Edward Thorndike and David Wechsler started to recognize the importance of non-intellective abilities. Thorndike described "social intelligence" as the ability to get along with others, a precursor to what we now understand as components of EQ.

However, it wasn't until the 1980s and 1990s that the term "emotional intelligence" became widely recognized. Researchers like Howard Gardner introduced the idea of multiple intelligences, which included both interpersonal (understanding others) and intrapersonal (understanding oneself) intelligences. But the concept truly gained traction with Daniel Goleman's 1995 book, "Emotional Intelligence," which highlighted EQ as a key factor in professional and personal success, often more so than traditional intelligence.

Today, emotional intelligence is acknowledged globally as a vital skill, with businesses, educational institutions, and leaders emphasizing its importance. The evolution of EQ from ancient philosophy to a recognized field of modern psychology demonstrates humanity's enduring interest in understanding and harnessing the power of our emotional world.

The Digital Age and Emotional Disconnect

The digital revolution has dramatically changed the landscape of human interaction. Today, it's possible to have a "conversation" with someone without ever hearing their voice or seeing their face. Platforms like Twitter, Instagram, and WhatsApp have redefined communication norms.

Research has shown that, despite being "hyper-connected," people, especially younger generations, report feeling lonelier than ever. A study from the University of Pennsylvania in 2018 found a correlation between high social media usage and feelings of loneliness and depression.

However, emotional intelligence can be a beacon in this digital fog. EQ equips individuals to read between the lines of text messages, to feel the emotions behind an emoji, and to recognize when someone needs more than just a "like" on their post. For instance, a person with developed EQ might sense emotional distress in a friend's vague social media post and reach out for a real conversation, bridging the digital-emotional divide.

Mental Health in a Fast-Paced World

Modern life often feels like a relentless sprint, where slowing down is equated with falling behind. A survey from the American Psychological Association highlighted that chronic stress, arising from work pressures to personal responsibilities, is a growing concern for many Americans.

Emotional intelligence doesn't just help in understanding and managing our emotions; it also aids in recognizing the emotional states of those around us. A colleague might be struggling with personal issues, or a friend might be facing professional challenges. EQ allows us to be sensitive to these nuances, offering support or space as needed.

Furthermore, emotional self-regulation, a component of EQ, provides tools for managing stress. Techniques like mindfulness meditation, guided imagery, or deep-breathing exercises, often rooted in emotional intelligence principles, have been shown to help individuals cope with the pressures of modern life.

EQ in the Modern Workplace

The value of EQ in professional settings cannot be overstated. A study by TalentSmart found that 90% of top performers in the workplace possess high EQ. These individuals navigate workplace dynamics more effectively, foster collaborative environments, and tend to be more adaptable to change.

Consider leadership, for instance. A leader with high EQ doesn't just give orders but understands team dynamics, recognizes individual strengths and weaknesses, and addresses conflicts with empathy and clarity. Such leaders are more likely to inspire loyalty, motivation, and innovation among their teams.

Additionally, emotional intelligence plays a pivotal role in customer relations. Companies like Apple or Zappos, known for their customer service, often train their employees in EQ principles to better understand and address customer needs and emotions.

The Role of EQ in Building Authentic Relationships

In an era where relationships can begin with a swipe on an app, the depth and authenticity of connections have become even more critical. High EQ individuals tend to be more attentive listeners, picking up on non-verbal cues and emotions often overlooked in conversation. This deepened understanding can form the foundation of lasting bonds.

For example, in romantic relationships, understanding a partner's emotional needs and responding empathetically can be the difference between a fleeting connection and a lifelong partnership. Similarly, parents with developed EQ can better comprehend the emotional struggles their children face in today's complex world, fostering trust and open communication.

Chapter 1: Understanding Emotions

Every emotion we experience can be likened to a symphony, with multiple instruments playing in harmony to create a collective sound. This complex web of factors that coalesce to form an emotion is both fascinating and enlightening when unraveled.

At the heart of our emotional responses lie our biological underpinnings. When an external event or internal thought sparks an emotion, our brain's specific regions, notably the amygdala, spring into action. These regions process the stimuli and instigate a cascade of neurochemical interactions. Neurotransmitters, the brain's chemical messengers, play a significant role here. The elation one might feel during a moment of success can be linked to a surge in dopamine, a neurotransmitter associated with pleasure and reward. In contrast, feelings of melancholy might emerge from a dip in serotonin levels.

However, emotions are not solely dictated by biology. Cognitive processes run parallel to these physiological reactions, shaping the texture and depth of what we feel. Our perceptions, beliefs, and past experiences act as filters, coloring our emotions with personal hues. For instance, a rainstorm might evoke feelings of sadness in someone who associates it with a past grief, while another person might find comfort in the rhythmic sound of raindrops, reminiscent of cherished memories.

Emotions also propel us into action. They manifest behaviorally, nudging us towards specific actions or reactions. The warmth of love might lead one to pen a heartfelt letter, while the sting of betrayal could cause withdrawal or confrontation. These urges, deeply embedded in our evolutionary history, once served critical survival functions. Our ancestors relied on the sharp jolt of fear to evade predators, and feelings of trust and camaraderie ensured group cohesion and mutual protection.

Our environment, culture, and upbringing further sculpt our emotional responses. Emotions are not universal in their expression; they are flavored by societal norms, traditions, and personal experiences. A celebration in one culture might involve solemn rituals, while in another, it might be marked by exuberant dancing. Likewise, the way emotions are perceived, valued, and expressed varies widely. In some societies, showing anger might be seen as a sign of weakness, while in others, it's a valid expression of dissent.

In essence, the anatomy of an emotion is a harmonious blend of biology, cognition, behavior, and environment. Each emotion, whether fleeting or profound, offers a window into this intricate dance, providing insights into our deepest desires, fears, values, and beliefs. By understanding the components that craft our emotions, we are better positioned to navigate the vast seas of our emotional worlds, making choices that resonate with our authentic selves.

Delving deeper into the intricate world of emotions allows us to appreciate the profound interplay of multiple factors that mold our feelings. When we experience an emotion, we're not merely feeling; we're engaging in a comprehensive dialogue between our past, present, environment, and inherent biology.

When a stimulus—be it a song, a memory, or a tactile sensation—triggers an emotion, our brain acts as the grand conductor. The amygdala, often referred to as the emotional center of the brain, assesses the stimulus. However, it doesn't work in isolation. The hippocampus, with its vault of memories, provides context. For example, the scent of jasmine might evoke nostalgia in one individual, reminding them of their grandmother's garden, while another might find it invigorating, associating it with a particular morning ritual.

As the brain processes the stimuli, a cascade of neurochemical events unfolds. These aren't just abstract chemical reactions; they're tangible experiences. A serotonin surge might feel like a blanket of contentment, while a rush of adrenaline could set our heart racing, preparing us for action. These neurochemicals shape the emotional landscape but are also influenced by various external factors. A lack of sunlight, for instance, can lead to reduced serotonin production, influencing mood.

Yet, emotions aren't just internal phenomena. They are deeply intertwined with our cognitive frameworks. Our beliefs, shaped over years of experiences and learnings, act as prisms, refracting emotional experiences. Someone who values independence might feel elated after buying their first car, seeing it as a symbol of autonomy. In contrast, another might view the same event with trepidation, overwhelmed by the responsibilities it brings.

The ripple effect of emotions extends to our behaviors. Emotions don't just exist in a vacuum; they urge us to act, to respond. The comfort of a close friend's presence might encourage sharing personal stories, while the anxiety of a looming deadline could result in focused work or, in some cases, procrastination.

The cultural milieu we're steeped in further textures our emotions. Cultures aren't just about languages or cuisines; they're repositories of collective emotional wisdom. In some Eastern cultures, for instance, collective joy or grief is encouraged, with emotions being a shared experience. In stark contrast, many Western societies prize individual emotional experiences, emphasizing personal exploration and expression.

At a more granular level, every emotion can be seen as a tapestry woven with threads of past encounters, societal norms, genetic predispositions, and current circumstances. A feeling isn't merely a fleeting reaction; it's a narrative, telling stories of ancient evolutionary needs, childhood memories, societal expectations, and immediate environments.

In the grand orchestra of our lives, emotions play the leading role, resonating with the melodies of our experiences and the rhythms of our surroundings. Understanding this intricate symphony allows us to not just hear, but truly listen to ourselves, fostering a richer, more nuanced relationship with our inner world.

Cultural Differences in Emotional Expression

Culture and emotions are so tightly interwoven that they often seem indistinguishable. Every society, with its unique traditions, norms, and values, imparts a distinct emotional language to its members. This language not only influences how emotions are felt but also how they're expressed and interpreted.

Across the globe, from bustling metropolises to secluded hamlets, emotions serve as the universal language. Yet, the dialects vary. Take the simple act of greeting, for example. In some cultures, it's common to greet with a hug or a kiss on the cheek, radiating warmth and affection. In others, a respectful bow or a firm handshake suffices, indicating mutual respect and acknowledgment.

The reasons behind these differences aren't merely based on tradition; they're rooted in deep-seated beliefs about self, society, and the relationship between the two. Individualistic societies, where personal autonomy and individual rights are emphasized, often promote open and direct emotional expression. People are encouraged to "speak their mind" and "follow their heart". Emotions like pride are celebrated as they align with individual achievement and personal success.

Conversely, collectivist cultures prioritize group harmony and societal cohesion. Here, emotions are often expressed in more subdued or indirect ways to maintain peace and avoid conflict. Emotions like shame have a significant role, as they can indicate a misalignment with group values or societal expectations.

Another fascinating dimension is the cultural script associated with certain emotions. Mourning, a universal human experience, is a poignant example. In some cultures, grief is expressed loudly and publicly, with community members joining the bereaved in their sorrow, making it a collective experience. In contrast, other societies may encourage a more private mourning process, emphasizing quiet reflection and personal memories.

However, these cultural norms don't just dictate expression; they influence emotional perception. An American might view an enthusiastic agreement with a nod and a smile as genuine, while a Japanese individual might interpret the same gesture as a mere form of politeness, devoid of deep agreement.

Emotional intelligence, in a multicultural world, thus becomes a nuanced dance. It's about understanding not just one's own emotional language but also appreciating the diverse dialects of emotions worldwide. This doesn't mean we need to know every cultural nuance, but it does highlight the importance of approaching emotional interactions with an open mind and a willingness to learn.

In essence, cultural differences in emotional expression offer a window into the vast tapestry of human experience. By understanding and appreciating these variations, we enrich our own emotional vocabulary, fostering deeper connections and promoting mutual respect across different walks of life.

Emotions have been humanity's compass throughout our evolutionary journey. They've warned us of danger, attracted us to potential partners, and fostered social cohesion. Yet, the way these emotions are expressed and interpreted varies dramatically across cultures, shaped by millennia of historical, environmental, and societal influences.

For instance, consider the concept of "honor" and its emotional connotations. In many Middle Eastern, Mediterranean, and Asian cultures, honor isn't just about personal pride; it's interwoven with family reputation and societal standing. Any perceived slight or disrespect can evoke strong emotional reactions, not only from the individual concerned but also from their family and community. This collective sentiment traces back to ancient tribal and clan systems where an affront to one was deemed an affront to all. The emotional intensity around honor in these cultures has shaped various customs, legal systems, and even art forms.

In contrast, let's look at the Scandinavian concept of "lagom", often translated as "just the right amount." Rooted in Viking societal norms and further shaped by the harsh Nordic environment, lagom emphasizes moderation, balance, and community over individualism. Emotionally, this translates to a preference for calm, understated expressions and a deep-seated discomfort with extremes, be it extreme joy, anger, or sorrow. The emotional restraint celebrated in these societies is not indicative of emotional lack but rather a different emotional calibration.

Another illuminating lens is the difference in emotional display rules across cultures. "Display rules" are cultural norms that dictate how, when, and where it's appropriate to express certain emotions. In many East Asian cultures, for instance, open displays of anger or frustration, especially towards elders or in public settings, are frowned upon. Instead, emotions might be channeled through art, poetry, or private reflection. This is not repression, but rather a cultural choice of emotional expression which values harmony and societal cohesion.

However, globalization and the digital age are blurring these cultural emotional boundaries. The advent of global media, international travel, and cross-cultural interactions is leading to a fascinating amalgamation and sometimes clash of emotional norms. A young Indian professional working in a multinational corporation might grapple with integrating the Western emphasis on assertiveness and individual expression with the Indian cultural script of respect for hierarchy and indirect communication.

Moreover, as societies evolve and diversify, there's an increasing recognition that within any given culture, emotional expressions can vary based on gender, age, class, and personal experiences. The emotional world of a young urban Japanese woman might differ significantly from that of her grandmother, even though they share cultural roots.

In conclusion, understanding cultural differences in emotional expression isn't just academic; it's a pathway to deeper human connection. By appreciating the rich tapestry of emotional dialects across the world, we not only foster mutual respect but also enrich our own emotional landscape, learning that at the heart of it all, emotions are our shared human heritage.

Positive vs. Negative Emotions: A Spectrum

Emotions, like colors, come in a vast array of shades and intensities. In the realm of psychology and everyday discourse, we often categorize emotions into two broad domains: positive and negative. However, such categorization, while convenient, might not capture the intricate nature and the interconnectedness of our emotional experiences.

When we think of positive emotions, joy, love, gratitude, and hope often come to mind. These emotions uplift us, motivating us to connect, share, and celebrate. They're associated with an expansion of our thought-action repertoire, enabling us to think creatively, solve problems, and bond with others. For instance, the sensation of happiness isn't just a fleeting moment of pleasure; it's evolution's way of reinforcing behaviors that, historically, might have contributed to our survival, such as cooperation, bonding, or exploring new environments.

Negative emotions, on the other hand, like fear, anger, sadness, or jealousy, often feel unpleasant. Yet, they too have their evolutionary purpose. Fear, for instance, heightens our senses and prepares us for flight or fight, historically keeping us safe from predators. Sadness might make us slow down and reflect, often signaling to others that we need support. Anger can serve as a clarion call for justice, prompting us to address wrongs and set boundaries.

However, labeling emotions as strictly positive or negative might be an oversimplification. Consider envy, typically deemed a negative emotion. While it might arise from feelings of inadequacy or longing, it can also be a catalyst for self-improvement and motivation. Similarly, excessive joy or excitement in inappropriate contexts, like schadenfreude (pleasure derived from someone else's misfortune), might not be entirely 'positive'.

The real value, perhaps, lies not in categorizing emotions but in understanding their origins, their purposes, and the messages they carry. Emotions are signals, and by tuning into these signals, we can navigate our lives more effectively. Instead of dismissing certain emotions as purely negative, we could approach them with curiosity. What is this anger teaching me? Is this sadness pointing towards an unmet need? By reframing our approach, we transform emotions from mere reactions to guides.

Furthermore, our emotions don't exist in silos. Joy can coexist with melancholy, leading to feelings of bittersweet nostalgia. Anxiety might be intertwined with excitement, as one might feel before a big presentation or performance. Recognizing this emotional interplay enriches our understanding and allows for a more compassionate approach towards ourselves and others.

In diverse cultures and personal contexts, the perception of what constitutes positive and negative can vary immensely. In some spiritual traditions, detachment from both joy and sorrow is seen as the path to inner peace, while in many modern societies, the relentless pursuit of happiness is often championed.

In conclusion, while the dichotomy of positive and negative emotions offers a starting point, the true spectrum of human emotion is vast, nuanced, and interwoven. Embracing this complexity provides a richer, more holistic understanding of ourselves and the world around us.

Delving further into the intricate dance of positive and negative emotions, it becomes clear that the human emotional landscape is far more intricate than a mere binary division.

Drawing inspiration from ancient Eastern philosophies, our emotions mirror the Yin and Yang concept. Just as these elements depict complementary opposites in harmony, emotions, too, possess counterparts and reflections. Joy carries with it a shadow of vulnerability, and behind the fiery façade of anger often lies concealed pain. It's this duality that adds depth and richness to our emotional experiences.

Furthermore, the nature of an emotion is not fixed; it's fluid, often shifting with context. Pride serves as a prime example. When stemming from personal achievements, it stands as a monument to hard work and perseverance. However, when intertwined with unchecked ego, the same pride can morph into arrogance, causing rifts in relationships and hindering personal growth.

It's also essential to recognize the transformative power of what we conventionally label as 'negative' emotions. Grief, with its weight of sorrow, can pave the way for profound personal growth, nurturing a deeper empathy and appreciation for the fleeting moments of life. Similarly, failures, despite their sting of disappointment, can become fertile grounds for resilience and newfound determination.

Modern societal norms, especially in the digital age of curated social media profiles, emphasize a continuous parade of happiness and success. This portrayal can sometimes cast shadows on the more challenging emotions, encouraging their suppression. Yet, true emotional well-being isn't about an endless pursuit of happiness; it's about embracing the entirety of our emotional spectrum, seeking authenticity and wholeness in our experiences.

Cultural and historical lenses further enhance the complexity of this spectrum. Ancient Greek dramas, for instance, revered the cathartic power of emotions like sorrow and fear, painting them as essential facets of the human experience. Indigenous cultures around the world have rituals where emotions like sadness aren't hidden away but are shared and processed communally, underlining the shared nature of human emotional experiences.

From the vast corridors of neuroscience, we glean insights into the intertwined nature of our emotions. The brain, in its intricate design, doesn't isolate positive and negative emotions into separate realms. Structures like the amygdala play pivotal roles in processing a range of emotions, from fear to pleasure, showcasing the profound interconnectedness of our emotional world.

In essence, while categorizations like 'positive' and 'negative' offer starting points for understanding emotions, true insight emerges when we dive deeper, exploring the myriad shades, reflections, and depths of our emotional existence.

Navigating the vast seas of our emotions is akin to embarking on an odyssey, where every wave, every ripple, carries its own story and meaning. Far from the static labels of 'positive' and 'negative', emotions are dynamic, shaping and being shaped by our lived experiences, memories, and the ever-evolving tapestry of human relationships.

Consider the nuanced emotion of nostalgia, which beautifully illustrates the interplay of joy and melancholy. Reminiscing about days gone by might bring a smile to our lips, even as a tinge of sadness touches our hearts for moments that will never return. This bittersweet sensation isn't strictly positive or negative—it's a complex brew of both, a testament to our capacity to feel multiple emotions simultaneously.

Furthermore, our surroundings and daily experiences continually influence our emotional state. A serene walk through nature can evoke feelings of awe and wonder, while the frantic pace of city life might stir stress and exhilaration in equal measure. The changing seasons, too, can mirror our inner emotional landscapes—the rejuvenation of spring might resonate with feelings of hope, while the quietude of winter might evoke introspection.

Moreover, our interpersonal connections act as powerful catalysts for our emotions. Human beings are inherently social creatures, and our relationships often serve as mirrors, reflecting back myriad emotions. A single conversation can traverse a spectrum of feelings, from curiosity to understanding, from disagreement to reconciliation. And it's through these interactions that we not only understand our own emotional depth but also develop empathy for others.

It's also worth noting how literature, art, and music play pivotal roles in exploring and expressing emotions. A poignant piece of music or a powerful line in a poem can evoke feelings that might have lain dormant, reminding us of the shared human experience across time and space. These artistic expressions serve as bridges, connecting us to emotions we might struggle to articulate otherwise.

The passage of time adds another layer to our emotional tapestry. As we age, our perspectives evolve, and emotions that once seemed overwhelming might now be met with equanimity. Conversely, moments of happiness from our youth might be viewed through rose-tinted glasses, their joy amplified by the sands of time.

The dynamism of emotions suggests that they aren't mere reactions to external stimuli but are deeply interwoven into the fabric of our being. They inform our decisions, shape our perceptions, and, in many ways, define our humanity. And while the journey through this emotional landscape is uniquely personal, it's also universally human, a voyage that each of us undertakes, discovering along the way the intricate dance of joy and sorrow, love and loss, and the countless shades in between.

Chapter 2: The Pillars of Emotional Intelligence

Emotional Intelligence, often abbreviated as EQ (Emotional Quotient), is akin to an ancient temple supported by grand pillars. Each pillar represents a facet of understanding and managing not just our emotions, but also those of others. As we venture deeper into the temple, we begin to see the intricate architecture of our emotional realm and the potential for growth that lies within.

The first pillar, **Self-Awareness**, is the cornerstone of emotional intelligence. Without a deep understanding of oneself, navigating the emotional world becomes akin to a ship sailing without a compass. Self-awareness involves not just recognizing our emotions as they arise but understanding their origins and implications. It's about being attuned to our inner world, noting the subtle shifts in mood, and discerning the difference between a fleeting feeling and a more profound emotional undercurrent. This pillar encourages introspection and reflection, urging us to ask ourselves why we feel a certain way and how these feelings influence our thoughts and actions.

Self-Management, the second pillar, builds upon the foundation of self-awareness. Recognizing our emotions is the first step; managing them is the journey. Self-management doesn't imply suppressing or denying our feelings. Instead, it emphasizes regulating and channeling them in constructive ways. It's the art of taking a deep breath before reacting in anger, or harnessing the energy of excitement without becoming reckless. It involves resilience in the face of adversity and the ability to bounce back from emotional setbacks.

Next, we encounter the pillar of **Social Awareness**. While the first two pillars focus inward, social awareness directs our attention outward, towards the people and environment around us. It's the ability to read the room, to sense the unspoken emotions in a conversation, and to understand the dynamics of group interactions. Empathy, a crucial component of social awareness, involves not just understanding but feeling what others feel, bridging the gap between individual experiences.

The final pillar, **Relationship Management**, is where emotional intelligence truly shines. Building and nurturing relationships require a delicate balance of self-awareness, self-management, and social awareness. It's about building trust, navigating conflicts with grace, and fostering genuine connections. Whether in personal or professional settings, effective relationship management can lead to collaborative and fulfilling interactions.

As we move through the vast hallways of this temple, illuminated by the wisdom of these pillars, we come to appreciate the profound impact of emotional intelligence on every facet of our lives. From personal relationships to professional success, from mental well-being to personal growth, EQ holds the keys to a deeper understanding and richer life experience. The journey through this temple is not a one-time venture but a lifelong exploration, as we continually learn, adapt, and grow in our emotional wisdom.

Self-Awareness

The Mirror of Self-Reflection

At the heart of self-awareness lies the practice of self-reflection. Like standing before a mirror, self-reflection offers us a candid view of our emotional self, beyond the layers of defense, rationalization, and ego. It's an intimate rendezvous with our innermost feelings, desires, fears, and aspirations.

Self-reflection is not merely about identifying emotions as they manifest; it delves deeper into understanding their origins. Why did a particular remark from a colleague stir feelings of insecurity? Why does a particular memory from childhood evoke such strong nostalgia? By pondering these questions, we begin to trace the pathways of our emotions, understanding the events, experiences, and beliefs that have shaped them.

While introspection provides clarity, it's equally vital to approach it with an open heart and mind. This means setting aside self-judgment and embracing vulnerability. It's about acknowledging emotions that might be uncomfortable or contradictory, recognizing that they are an inherent part of our complex emotional landscape. For instance, one might simultaneously experience love and resentment towards a family member or feel both excitement and dread for an upcoming event.

Another essential aspect of self-reflection is recognizing patterns in our emotional responses. Over time, through consistent introspection, we might notice that certain situations or triggers consistently evoke particular emotions. Maybe tight deadlines always induce stress, or spending time in nature invariably brings serenity. Recognizing these patterns is the first step towards managing them effectively.

Furthermore, self-reflection is closely intertwined with self-acceptance. As we delve deeper into our emotions, we must embrace them all, whether they be feelings of pride, moments of regret, or pangs of jealousy. Every emotion offers insight into our psyche, and by accepting them, we take ownership of our emotional journey.

Journaling can be a powerful tool in this journey of self-reflection. By putting thoughts to paper, we externalize our emotions, giving them form and structure. Over time, revisiting these journal entries can offer valuable insights into our emotional growth and transformation.

As we continuously engage with this mirror of self-reflection, we cultivate a profound understanding of ourselves. We become more attuned to our emotional ebbs and flows, better equipped to navigate the challenges of life with empathy and grace. This intimate knowledge of oneself lays the foundation for all other pillars of emotional intelligence, paving the way for a life of emotional depth and authenticity.

The Power of Introspection

Introspection, often considered synonymous with self-reflection, is more than just a mirror to one's emotions. It is a deep dive into the waters of one's mind, a conscious exploration of the myriad thoughts, beliefs, and impressions that shape our emotional landscape.

Introspection involves delving beneath the surface-level reactions to understand the core beliefs and values that drive our emotional responses. It asks us to pause and consider not just the "what" but the "why" behind our feelings. For instance, while self-reflection might help us recognize that we're feeling anxious about a presentation, introspection nudges us further, pushing us to explore why we associate presentations with anxiety. Is it a fear of judgment, a past experience where things went awry, or perhaps an internalized belief about our capabilities?

By understanding these deeper drivers, we empower ourselves to address the root causes rather than merely the symptoms of our emotional states. Over time, this can lead to transformative shifts in our emotional well-being.

Moreover, introspection is a gateway to mindfulness. By focusing our attention inward, we cultivate a heightened sense of present awareness. We become more attuned to the subtleties of our emotional experiences, noticing the transient nature of feelings and the triggers that might amplify or dampen them. This conscious attention creates a buffer against impulsive reactions, allowing us to respond to situations with greater clarity and intentionality.

While the process of introspection is deeply personal, it doesn't necessarily have to be a solitary one. Engaging in meaningful conversations with trusted individuals can provide valuable external perspectives. Sometimes, others can offer insights or observations that we might have overlooked or been too close to see. These exchanges can be illuminating, enriching our introspective journey with shared wisdom and experiences.

However, it's essential to approach introspection with patience. It's not always about finding immediate answers but about fostering a continuous dialogue with oneself. It's a journey of discovery, where each session of introspection might reveal another layer, another nuance of our emotional being.

In essence, introspection is the compass that guides us through the vast terrains of our inner world. By regularly consulting this compass, we not only deepen our understanding of ourselves but also refine our navigation skills, steering our lives with greater emotional intelligence and purpose.

Recognizing Emotional Triggers

In our daily lives, amidst a whirlwind of experiences and interactions, there are specific stimuli or events that elicit strong emotional responses within us. These are our emotional triggers. Much like a particular note can make a string vibrate in resonance, certain situations, words, or actions resonate within our emotional spectrum, evoking feelings that can sometimes be intense and overwhelming.

Understanding one's emotional triggers is a significant aspect of self-awareness. It's akin to knowing the weather patterns when setting sail on the sea. By recognizing what might stir up emotional tempests, we can better prepare and navigate through them.

Emotional triggers often have roots in past experiences, especially those from our formative years. An offhand remark by a colleague might bring back memories of being ridiculed in school, leading to feelings of anger or embarrassment in the present. Similarly, witnessing an act of kindness might remind one of a loved one's gestures, evoking feelings of warmth and nostalgia.

However, recognizing these triggers is just the beginning. It's essential to understand that while we might not always have control over the triggering event, we do possess the power to manage our response to it. For example, if one knows that criticism, even if constructive, is a trigger due to past experiences of harsh judgment, acknowledging this can help in framing a more measured and constructive response rather than a defensive or aggressive one.

Being aware of our triggers also enhances our empathy towards others. Just as we have our triggers, so does everyone else. Recognizing this universality helps in fostering understanding and patience in interpersonal interactions. If someone reacts strongly to a seemingly innocuous statement, it might very well be a trigger for them, rooted in their personal history.

Regular introspection and self-reflection can aid in identifying these triggers. Over time, patterns emerge, revealing consistent emotional responses to specific stimuli. With this knowledge, one can work on strategies to address and manage these triggers. This might involve cognitive reframing, where one consciously changes the narrative around the triggering event, or it might involve seeking therapeutic interventions to address deep-rooted triggers.

In the grand tapestry of emotional intelligence, understanding our triggers is like knowing the knots and threads that bind the fabric together. By recognizing and addressing them, we ensure that our emotional fabric remains resilient, vibrant, and reflective of our authentic selves.

Self-Management

Strategies for Emotional Regulation

Emotions are like the ever-changing tides of the ocean - at times calm and serene, at other moments turbulent and overpowering. While it's impossible to halt the ebb and flow of the waves, with the right strategies, we can learn to surf them with grace and skill. This is the essence of emotional regulation, a pivotal aspect of self-management.

At its core, emotional regulation is not about suppressing or stifling emotions. Instead, it revolves around acknowledging, understanding, and channeling them in ways that align with our values, goals, and well-being. Just as a musician doesn't silence an instrument but learns to play it harmoniously, we must learn to harmonize our emotional symphony.

The first step in this journey is the acceptance of the full range of our emotions. Every emotion, whether joy, anger, sadness, or excitement, has its place and purpose in our emotional repertoire. They are signals, conveying messages about our internal state and external environment. For instance, anger might signal a boundary being crossed, while sadness might point to a loss or unmet need. By accepting and understanding these signals, we equip ourselves to address the underlying causes rather than getting lost in the emotion itself.

However, understanding alone isn't sufficient. The real mastery of emotional regulation comes when we develop strategies to navigate these emotional waters effectively. One such strategy is the practice of grounding. When overwhelmed by a strong emotion, grounding techniques, like focusing on one's breath or physical sensations, can help anchor us in the present moment, providing a momentary reprieve from the emotional storm and allowing us to respond rather than react.

Another powerful tool for emotional regulation is cognitive reframing. Our emotions are often influenced by our perceptions and beliefs about a situation. By challenging and changing these perceptions, we can shift our emotional response. For instance, viewing a setback not as a failure but as a learning opportunity can transform feelings of despair into determination.

Visualization can also play a pivotal role. Picturing a calming scene or remembering a happy memory can act as a counterbalance to distressing emotions, helping to bring equilibrium.

However, it's crucial to recognize that emotional regulation is a dynamic process. There's no one-size-fits-all strategy, and what works in one situation might not be as effective in another. It's about continuous learning and adaptation, refining our strategies based on experiences and feedback.

Moreover, seeking external support, whether through friends, family, or professional counselors, can be invaluable. They can offer perspective, validation, and strategies that we might not have considered.

In the vast landscape of our emotional lives, emotional regulation acts as our compass and map, guiding us through the peaks and valleys, ensuring that no matter how strong the emotion, we remain the master navigators of our emotional journey. With practice, patience, and perseverance, we can harness the power of our emotions, channeling them towards growth, fulfillment, and well-being.

The Role of Resilience

In the ever-evolving journey of emotional intelligence, resilience stands as a beacon of strength, helping us endure and adapt in the face of adversity. Much like the bamboo that bends under the force of a storm only to bounce back once it has passed, resilience ensures that we are not broken by the emotional storms we face, but instead, emerge stronger, wiser, and more adaptable.

Resilience is not merely about bouncing back; it's about growing through challenges. Every emotional setback or hardship carries with it lessons, insights, and opportunities for growth. A resilient individual doesn't just recover from these challenges but integrates the experiences, evolving in their understanding and emotional capabilities.

It's important to note that resilience is not an inherent trait that some possess and others lack. It's a cultivated skill, honed through experiences, mindset, and deliberate practice. The foundational stone of resilience is the belief in one's ability to cope. This self-efficacy, the belief in one's capabilities, acts as a shield, cushioning against feelings of helplessness when faced with adversity.

Connected to this is the art of positive reframing. Resilient individuals have a knack for viewing challenges from a broader perspective. They recognize that setbacks are temporary, that there's a larger narrative at play, and that with effort and persistence, obstacles can be overcome. They tend to see challenges as puzzles to be solved rather than insurmountable walls.

Another key facet of resilience is the cultivation of a strong emotional support system. Human beings are inherently social creatures, and our connections with others provide solace, perspective, and strength. In times of emotional turmoil, having someone to lean on, share with, or simply be there, can make a significant difference. These bonds of trust and understanding act as anchors, grounding us when emotional waves threaten to sweep us away.

Yet, it's also essential to develop a sense of inner sanctuary – a space of calm and solace within oneself. This could be through practices like meditation, journaling, or even simply spending quiet moments in nature. Such practices nurture a sense of inner peace, a reservoir of calm to tap into during challenging times.

Furthermore, embracing a growth mindset is integral to resilience. This means viewing challenges and setbacks not as defining judgments of one's capabilities but as opportunities for growth, learning, and evolution. With this mindset, even failures become stepping stones, each teaching valuable lessons and paving the way for future successes.

In the intricate dance of emotions, resilience is our rhythm, allowing us to sway with grace, no matter how intense the music. It ensures that we don't lose our footing, guiding us with the confidence that after every night, no matter how dark, there's the promise of dawn. As we cultivate resilience, we not only enhance our capacity to manage our emotions but also enrich our lives with depth, purpose, and enduring joy.

Overcoming Emotional Impulses

Our emotional landscape is punctuated with sudden impulses, akin to sudden gusts of wind that can quickly change our direction. These impulses, if unchecked, can lead to reactions that we might later regret, be it a hasty word uttered in anger or a decision made in the throes of passion. In the context of emotional intelligence, the ability to recognize and manage these impulses is essential, not just for harmonious interpersonal interactions, but also for our personal growth and well-being.

Emotional impulses are deeply rooted in our evolutionary history. They are quick, automatic reactions designed for immediate response, especially in situations perceived as threats. In the ancient days, these impulses served us well, preparing us to fight or flee in the face of danger. However, in our contemporary world, where threats are more psychological than physical, these impulses often become maladaptive, leading to overreactions or inappropriate responses.

The first step in managing these impulses is awareness. We must be attuned to the early signs of an emotional surge. It could be a tightening in the chest, a rush of heat, a sudden surge of energy, or any other physiological signal. Recognizing these signs provides a critical window, albeit brief, to pause and choose our response rather than being swept away by the impulse.

During this pause, one effective technique is to engage in deep breathing. It serves as an anchor, grounding us in the present moment. Breathing deeply not only has a calming effect on the nervous system but also gives us a moment to reflect, allowing the initial intensity of the impulse to subside.

Another strategy is to develop a mental space of observation. Instead of immediately identifying with the emotion, we can try to observe it as an outsider. This detachment allows us to see the emotion for what it is – a transient state, not a permanent part of our identity. By doing so, we gain perspective and reduce the urge to act impulsively.

It's also beneficial to cultivate a habit of reflection. By regularly reviewing situations where we acted on impulse, we can identify patterns, triggers, and typical reactions. This retrospective insight becomes a valuable tool in preempting and managing future impulsive reactions.

Furthermore, managing our environment and exposure can also aid in reducing emotional impulsivity. If certain situations, people, or stimuli consistently evoke strong impulses, it might be wise to limit exposure or develop specific strategies to handle them. For example, if heated debates often lead to anger, setting ground rules for discussions or taking regular breaks can be helpful.

Lastly, patience and self-compassion are crucial. Overcoming emotional impulses is a journey, and there will be times when we falter. Instead of being overly critical, acknowledging our humanity and treating ourselves with kindness can make the path of emotional mastery smoother.

In the rich tapestry of our emotional lives, impulses are vibrant, spontaneous strokes of color. While they add depth and spontaneity, unchecked, they can overshadow the subtler hues. By learning to manage these impulses, we ensure that our emotional artwork is balanced, harmonious, and truly representative of our authentic selves.

Social Awareness

The Art of Empathy

Empathy, often considered the cornerstone of social awareness, is the ability to deeply understand and share the feelings of another. It's like an emotional bridge that allows us to connect with others on a profound level, enabling us to perceive the world from their viewpoint, feeling their joys, their fears, their hopes, and their disappointments. This shared emotional resonance is vital, not just for building and maintaining relationships but also for fostering understanding, compassion, and unity in a diverse and interconnected world.

Empathy diverges from mere sympathy. While sympathy can be seen as feeling compassion for someone or recognizing their distress, empathy delves deeper, immersing us in the emotional experience of the other. It's not just recognizing that someone is sad; it's feeling a touch of that sadness with them.

The roots of empathy can be traced back to our evolutionary past. As social beings, humans have thrived in communities, and understanding the emotional states of those around us was crucial for survival and cooperation. Today, while the context has evolved, empathy remains essential for building trust, resolving conflicts, and fostering social cohesion.

Cultivating empathy begins with active listening. In our fast-paced world, truly listening to someone, without forming judgments or crafting responses in our minds, has become a rare skill. Active listening involves being fully present, paying attention to not just the spoken words but also to non-verbal cues, the tone of voice, facial expressions, and body language. It's about immersing oneself in the narrative of the other, seeking to understand their story deeply.

Empathy also involves a keen sense of curiosity. By genuinely being interested in the lives, experiences, and feelings of others, we open ourselves to understanding them better. It's about asking open-ended questions, seeking to delve deeper into their emotional landscape, and truly appreciating the uniqueness of their experience.

Empathy is also intertwined with vulnerability. To truly connect with someone, we often have to reveal a bit of our own emotional world, sharing our feelings, experiences, and perspectives. This mutual exchange of emotional truths strengthens the bond of understanding and trust.

However, while empathy is a beautiful and connecting emotion, it's essential to strike a balance. Being continuously immersed in the emotions of others can be overwhelming and can lead to empathy fatigue. Setting emotional boundaries, recognizing when to step back, and practicing self-care are crucial for ensuring that our empathetic engagements are sustainable and enriching.

In the realm of social awareness, empathy shines brightly as a beacon, illuminating the path to deeper connections, richer understanding, and a world where, despite our many differences, we recognize and honor our shared humanity. Through the art of empathy, we weave threads of connection, creating a tapestry of mutual respect, appreciation, and togetherness.

Reading Emotional Cues

Emotional cues are subtle signals, both verbal and non-verbal, that indicate an individual's emotional state. They are the silent language of feelings, conveying information that often goes beyond words. In a world filled with noise, being adept at reading these cues is fundamental to understanding others and navigating the intricate maze of human interactions.

Every day, we emit a myriad of emotional cues, often without even realizing it. A slight change in tone, a fleeting look of discomfort, a nervous fidget, or a warm, lingering smile – all these are tiny windows into our internal emotional world. And while these cues can sometimes be ambiguous or misinterpreted, when read in context and with attention, they provide invaluable insights into a person's feelings, needs, and intentions.

To truly decipher these cues, one must first be attuned to the present moment. In our digital age, with its relentless stream of notifications, messages, and distractions, being genuinely present during interactions has become a rare gift. It means fully engaging with the person, undivided by other concerns or thoughts. This focused attention becomes the foundation upon which the subtle nuances of emotional cues become noticeable.

However, presence alone is not enough. A deep-seated curiosity and genuine interest in the other person enhance our ability to perceive and interpret emotional signals. This means actively seeking to understand the layers beneath the surface, probing gently with questions or reflections, and being patient enough to listen, not just to words, but to the silences between them.

Cultural awareness also plays a significant role. Emotional cues are deeply embedded in cultural contexts. What might be considered a sign of respect in one culture could be perceived as indifference in another. Thus, understanding the cultural background and norms of the individual can provide a clearer lens through which to interpret their emotional cues.

It's also essential to recognize our own biases and assumptions. Sometimes, our past experiences, beliefs, or preconceived notions can color our interpretation of emotional cues. Being aware of these biases and constantly questioning our interpretations ensures that we remain objective and open to multiple perspectives.

Practicing self-reflection is another crucial aspect. By understanding our own emotional cues and recognizing how they manifest in various situations, we gain better insight into how to read others'. This self-awareness, combined with regular feedback from trusted individuals, refines our emotional cue reading capabilities over time.

However, with all this understanding, it's paramount to approach the process with humility. Even the most astute reader of emotional cues can sometimes misinterpret signals. When in doubt, it's always best to ask, to communicate, seeking clarity rather than making assumptions.

In the dance of human interaction, emotional cues are the rhythm guiding our steps. By becoming adept at reading them, we not only enhance our social awareness but also foster deeper, more meaningful connections. These connections, built on understanding and mutual respect, enrich our lives, bridging gaps, healing wounds, and bringing us closer in the shared journey of human experience.

Navigating Social Dynamics

Every society and community possesses an intricate web of unspoken rules, expectations, and relationships. Within this web, navigating social dynamics becomes an essential skill, allowing individuals to coexist harmoniously, understand underlying tensions, and foster deeper connections.

Social dynamics refer to the behavior of groups and the interactions and relationships between individuals within those groups. Whether it's in a family gathering, a professional meeting, or a casual outing with friends, understanding the flow of these dynamics can greatly enhance one's social experience.

Awareness of one's own emotions and how they influence behavior is the first step in understanding larger social currents. When we are aware of our feelings and how they drive our actions, we can better anticipate the reactions of others and adjust our behavior accordingly.

Further, every individual we interact with brings a set of beliefs, experiences, and emotions to the table. Acknowledging this diversity and approaching interactions with an open mind can lead to more enriching and less confrontational exchanges. It's essential to understand that while our perspective is valid, so are the perspectives of others. This mutual respect forms the foundation of positive social dynamics.

Active listening plays a significant role in this realm. Often, we're so engrossed in framing our next statement that we don't truly listen to what's being said. By genuinely hearing and processing another's words, we not only show respect but also gain insights into their mindset, facilitating smoother interactions.

The role of non-verbal communication in social dynamics cannot be understated. A significant portion of our communication is relayed through body language, facial expressions, and tone of voice. Being attuned to these subtle cues can provide a clearer understanding of the emotions and sentiments that words might not capture.

Social dynamics also encompass the larger cultural and societal norms that influence individual behavior. Being aware of these norms, especially when interacting with individuals from diverse backgrounds, ensures that communication remains respectful and avoids unintentional offense.

Conflict, while often viewed negatively, is a natural part of social interactions. How one navigates conflicts can significantly influence social dynamics. Approaching disagreements with an intent to understand rather than win, seeking common ground, and respecting differing viewpoints can turn conflicts into opportunities for growth and deeper connection.

Lastly, the ability to adapt and adjust is vital. While consistency is valuable, being too rigid in our interactions can lead to friction. Recognizing when to stand firm and when to be flexible can greatly enhance the flow of social dynamics, ensuring harmony and mutual respect.

In the dance of human interactions, understanding the steps, rhythms, and patterns is crucial. Navigating social dynamics with grace, empathy, and awareness enriches our experiences, fostering connections that are deep, genuine, and lasting.

Relationship Management

Building Trust and Rapport

Trust is the cornerstone of any meaningful relationship, whether personal or professional. It's the invisible thread that binds people together, creating a safe space for vulnerability, open communication, and mutual respect. While the significance of trust is universally acknowledged, the journey to cultivate and maintain it is intricate and demands conscious effort.

In the context of relationship management, building trust and rapport is not a one-time event but an ongoing process. It begins with the very first interaction and evolves over time, shaped by shared experiences, challenges, and moments of understanding.

Authenticity is the foundation upon which trust is built. People are more inclined to trust someone who presents themselves genuinely, without facades or pretensions. Being genuine means staying true to one's beliefs and values while also being open to listening and understanding others. It's a delicate balance between asserting oneself and respecting the boundaries and views of another.

Open and honest communication further fortifies trust. When individuals feel heard and valued, it fosters a sense of belonging and understanding. It's crucial to express one's feelings, concerns, and aspirations transparently, avoiding hidden agendas or concealed motives. Equally important is the willingness to listen actively, ensuring that conversations are two-sided and mutually enriching.

Reliability plays a significant role in building trust. Consistency in actions and words assures others of one's dependability. If promises are made, they should be kept. Even in situations where commitments can't be met, communicating proactively and offering explanations can help in maintaining the trust that's been established.

Empathy is another pivotal component in the equation of trust. Demonstrating genuine care and concern for others, understanding their perspectives, and valuing their emotions solidifies the bonds of trust. It signifies that the relationship is not merely transactional but is rooted in mutual respect and understanding.

Building rapport goes hand in hand with trust. It involves creating a connection, often facilitated by finding common ground or shared interests. Simple gestures, like remembering personal details or checking in on someone's well-being, can significantly enhance rapport. In essence, rapport is the feeling of comfort and camaraderie that emerges when individuals resonate with each other.

It's also essential to acknowledge that trust, once broken, can be challenging to rebuild. While not impossible, it requires concerted effort, patience, and, often, time. Regular reflections on one's actions, seeking feedback, and making amends when necessary can aid in mending trust.

In the intricate dance of relationships, trust and rapport are the rhythm that guides our steps. Cultivating them not only ensures harmonious interactions but also creates a foundation for deep, fulfilling, and enduring connections. Through conscious effort, understanding, and time, trust and rapport can become the pillars upon which lasting relationships stand.

Navigating Conflicts

Conflicts, whether subtle disagreements or pronounced disputes, are an inevitable aspect of human relationships. Rather than being feared or avoided, conflicts can be perceived as valuable opportunities for growth, understanding, and strengthening bonds. The way we approach and navigate these moments can significantly impact the trajectory of our relationships and the quality of our interpersonal dynamics.

Every conflict begins with an underlying difference - it could be a difference in perspective, values, expectations, or desires. Recognizing and understanding this divergence is the first step towards resolution. More often than not, conflicts arise not from the actual difference but from the perception of that difference, and the emotions and misunderstandings that ensue.

Active listening is a crucial tool in conflict navigation. Before crafting a response or defense, it's vital to truly hear and comprehend the other person's viewpoint. It's not just about the words spoken, but also the emotions and sentiments underlying them. Listening without immediately judging or countering allows for a space where both parties feel valued and understood.

Open communication, characterized by honesty and transparency, helps in shedding light on the roots of the conflict. When individuals express their feelings, concerns, and needs openly, it reduces ambiguity and helps in arriving at a common understanding. It's important to frame statements in a way that conveys one's feelings without blaming or accusing the other person.

Empathy, as in many aspects of relationship management, plays a pivotal role. By placing oneself in the other person's shoes, it becomes easier to grasp their emotions and motivations. This doesn't necessarily mean agreeing with them, but understanding where they are coming from can pave the way for a middle ground.

It's also crucial to remain solution-focused. Dredging up past grievances or deviating from the current issue at hand can further complicate matters. By concentrating on finding a resolution that is acceptable to all parties involved, the conflict becomes an avenue for progression rather than a roadblock.

Sometimes, taking a break or stepping back can be beneficial. If emotions run too high, it might be challenging to engage productively. A short respite can offer a fresh perspective and allow emotions to settle, making it easier to approach the issue with a clear mind.

Lastly, conflicts should be seen as learning opportunities. They shed light on areas of improvement, offer insights into the dynamics of the relationship, and often lead to deeper mutual understanding. By navigating conflicts with maturity, patience, and empathy, they can be transformed from sources of tension to catalysts for growth and connection.

Sustaining Long-Term Connections

Deep-rooted, enduring connections aren't mere happenstance; they're a culmination of continuous effort, understanding, and mutual growth. While the initial stages of a relationship might be fueled by the excitement of discovery and the thrill of the unknown, sustaining such connections over extended periods demands consistent nurturing and evolution.

A core component of long-lasting relationships is mutual respect. As individuals grow, change, and evolve, the respect for each other's journeys, decisions, and life choices remains paramount. Respecting boundaries, understanding limitations, and valuing the other's autonomy ensures that the connection retains its vitality even amidst challenges.

Adaptability is another cornerstone. As time progresses, circumstances change, individuals evolve, and what once was might no longer hold true. The flexibility to adapt, recalibrate, and refashion the dynamics of the relationship based on the current context is essential.

This adaptability is not about losing oneself but about molding the relationship to best suit the present moment, ensuring its continued relevance and strength.

Open and transparent communication, a recurring theme in relationship management, is especially vital here. Over time, it's natural for desires, expectations, and feelings to shift. Regularly checking in, expressing these changes, and actively listening to the other person's shifts fosters understanding and reduces potential friction. Such communication acts as the relationship's heartbeat, keeping it alive and vibrant.

Shared experiences play a crucial role in sustaining connections. These experiences, whether they're joyous celebrations, challenges overcome together, or simple everyday moments, weave the fabric of the relationship. They become the stories and memories that anchor the bond, providing a reservoir of shared history to revisit and cherish.

Another essential element is the commitment to mutual growth. As individuals progress in their personal journeys, supporting each other's aspirations, dreams, and endeavors becomes vital. This mutual growth isn't just about personal aspirations but also about growing together as a unit, seeking ways to enrich the relationship and ensuring that it remains a source of joy, support, and fulfillment.

Rekindling the spark is important, especially in relationships that span years or decades. This involves revisiting the elements that initially drew individuals together, recreating cherished memories, and continually finding new ways to celebrate and enjoy the connection.

Lastly, forgiveness and understanding play pivotal roles. In the vast expanse of a long-term relationship, misunderstandings, mistakes, and conflicts are inevitable. The willingness to forgive, understand the imperfections, and focus on the bigger picture ensures that minor hiccups don't overshadow the profound bond shared.

In essence, sustaining long-term connections is a dance of balance, understanding, and evolution. It demands effort, but the reward – a relationship that stands the test of time, offering unwavering support, joy, and companionship – is immeasurable. Through conscious nurturing, mutual respect, and continuous growth, these connections can thrive, shining brightly as beacons of human connection and understanding.

Chapter 3: The Connection between EQ and IQ

In the vast landscape of human intelligence, two dimensions often emerge as central: Emotional Intelligence (EQ) and Intellectual Intelligence (IQ). While both play significant roles in shaping our interactions, decision-making, and overall life experiences, understanding their interplay and distinct natures can offer profound insights into human potential and behavior.

At its core, IQ, or Intellectual Intelligence, pertains to cognitive abilities. It relates to our capacity to process information, solve problems, exhibit logical reasoning, and grasp complex ideas. Historically, IQ has been a favored metric in educational settings, used to gauge academic potential and predict future success. The conventional belief has often been that a higher IQ equates to better academic performance, job opportunities, and even higher earnings. Over the decades, numerous tests have been designed to measure IQ, aiming to quantify an individual's intellectual prowess.

Contrastingly, EQ, or Emotional Intelligence, delves into the realm of emotions and how individuals recognize, understand, manage, and express them. As previously discussed, it encompasses self-awareness, self-management, social awareness, and relationship management. Unlike IQ, which remains relatively stable throughout life, EQ can be developed and refined with conscious effort and practice.

The debate over which holds more importance in determining life success – EQ or IQ – has been longstanding. And while it's tempting to position one above the other, the reality is far more nuanced. It's not a matter of either-or but a symbiosis between the two.

For instance, consider the world of work. While specific professions might demand a high IQ – think of theoretical physicists or mathematicians – the ability to work within a team, communicate effectively, handle stress, and navigate workplace dynamics (all aspects of EQ) are equally crucial. In leadership roles, particularly, EQ often emerges as a determining factor for success. Leaders with high EQ can inspire, motivate, and understand their team, fostering a positive and productive work environment.

Conversely, in personal relationships, while EQ is paramount in ensuring harmonious and deep connections, IQ plays a role too. Intellectual compatibility, shared interests, and stimulating discussions can significantly enhance the depth and satisfaction derived from personal bonds.

Another fascinating aspect is how emotions can influence cognitive processes. For instance, an individual experiencing intense emotions – whether positive like elation or negative like distress – might find it challenging to concentrate or make logical decisions. Emotions can either cloud judgment or, when channeled correctly, can enhance creativity and problem-solving.

It's also worth noting the role of education and upbringing in shaping EQ and IQ. While traditional education systems have primarily focused on fostering IQ, the rising awareness about the importance of emotional well-being is slowly integrating EQ development into curriculums. The holistic development of a child entails nurturing both these intelligences, enabling them to navigate the complexities of life adeptly.

In essence, the relationship between EQ and IQ is intricate and interwoven. They're two facets of the multifaceted gem of human intelligence. While they have their distinct domains, their interplay is undeniable. Together, they shape our experiences, decisions, relationships, and, ultimately, our destinies. Recognizing their unique strengths and fostering both can lead to a more balanced, fulfilling, and enriched life.

Origins and Definitions: EQ vs. IQ

The origins of the concepts of IQ and EQ take us on a journey through the history of psychology and the evolution of our understanding of human intelligence.

The concept of an intelligence quotient or IQ can be traced back to the early 20th century. Alfred Binet, a French psychologist, was among the pioneers who developed the first intelligence test. Binet's primary goal was to identify school children in need of special assistance in academics. His test was constructed to assess various cognitive abilities such as memory, attention, and problem-solving skills. The term "intelligence quotient" emerged from the method of scoring this test – a division of the 'mental age' by the 'chronological age'. Thus, IQ became a standardized measure to gauge cognitive abilities.

Over time, the IQ test evolved, with different versions and modifications tailored to various populations and age groups. The emphasis largely remained on cognitive and logical skills, with the underlying assumption that these were primary indicators of potential success in academic and professional realms.

In contrast, the formal acknowledgment of Emotional Intelligence as a distinct form of intelligence is relatively recent. The term gained significant traction in the 1990s, especially with the publication of Daniel Goleman's book "Emotional Intelligence." However, the seeds of the concept can be found much earlier in Howard Gardner's theory of multiple intelligences proposed in the 1980s. Gardner introduced the idea that intelligence wasn't a monolithic entity but had various facets, including interpersonal and intrapersonal intelligences, which laid the groundwork for what we now recognize as EQ.

While IQ focuses on tasks such as pattern recognition, mathematical abilities, and linguistic skills, EQ emphasizes self-awareness, empathy, motivation, self-regulation, and social skills. It's a measure of our capacity to be aware of, control, and express our emotions and to handle interpersonal relationships judiciously and empathetically.

The distinction between the two is also evident in their developmental trajectories. While cognitive intelligence or IQ tends to stabilize as we enter adulthood, emotional intelligence is more malleable, allowing for growth and development throughout life. This plasticity of EQ offers hope and opportunity for individuals to refine and enhance their emotional skills at any age.

As the modern world becomes more interconnected and socially complex, the significance of EQ has come to the forefront. In professional settings, while technical skills and cognitive abilities remain important, soft skills — primarily governed by EQ — are becoming increasingly valued. These include leadership qualities, teamwork, communication skills, and adaptability.

In conclusion, while EQ and IQ originate from different philosophical and historical backgrounds, and serve different functions, their combined influence on an individual's life is profound. An optimal balance of both allows for a comprehensive understanding of the world, both intellectually and emotionally, and equips individuals with the tools to thrive in varied environments and circumstances.

The Interplay between Emotion and Logic

The interplay between emotion and logic is one of the most intricate dynamics governing human behavior. This dance, between what we feel and what we think, often determines our decisions, our actions, and even our sense of identity. Exploring this relationship provides profound insights into the human psyche and can be the key to a deeper understanding of our motivations and actions.

Historically, emotion and logic have been perceived as opposing forces. From the time of ancient philosophers like Plato, who regarded reason as superior, to the modern era where logic-driven decisions are often praised, there has been a bias towards rationality. Emotions, on the other hand, have been viewed as turbulent, impulsive, and even capricious—qualities that could cloud judgment and lead to irrational actions.

However, this perspective has begun to shift with advances in neuroscience and psychology. Modern research suggests that emotion and logic are not antagonistic; rather, they work in tandem, complementing and influencing each other. Far from being enemies, they are partners in the decision-making process.

At the neurological level, emotion and reason are intertwined. The brain's limbic system, especially the amygdala, is responsible for processing emotions. In contrast, the prefrontal cortex is crucial for higher-order cognitive functions and rational decision-making. While these areas have distinct roles, they are interconnected, allowing for continuous communication. When faced with a decision, emotional responses are almost instantaneous, giving the first 'gut feeling' or instinctive reaction. The logical processes, being a tad slower, weigh in next, evaluating the situation based on facts, past experiences, and possible outcomes.

One might wonder why emotions are often our first response. From an evolutionary perspective, emotions provided our ancestors with immediate reactions to threats or opportunities, ensuring survival. For example, fear in response to a lurking predator or joy at finding a food source were essential emotions that guided immediate and life-saving actions.

However, as human societies grew complex, mere emotional responses were not sufficient. Situations demanded analysis, foresight, and planning—enter logic and reason. While emotions ensured immediate survival, logic became the tool for long-term survival, helping our ancestors strategize, build societies, and create civilizations.

Yet, emotions never lost their significance. They became the basis for our values, our passions, and even our sense of purpose. Love, compassion, and empathy, though emotional, became the bedrock of social cohesion. Emotions gave life color, depth, and meaning.

The true power lies in harnessing both emotion and logic. Consider a situation where a person has to decide between a high-paying job that they don't resonate with and a lesser-paying job that aligns with their passion. Emotionally, they might be drawn to the latter, feeling a sense of joy and fulfillment at the thought. Logically, considering financial security, growth prospects, and societal expectations, the former might seem a better choice. A decision that balances both these perspectives would be the most holistic, taking into account immediate emotional well-being and long-term considerations.

In everyday life, recognizing the interplay between emotion and logic can lead to more informed, balanced decisions. It helps in understanding that emotions are not irrational but are data points indicating our values, beliefs, and desires. Logic, on the other hand, provides structure, clarity, and a roadmap. Together, they create a compass that not only guides but also enriches the journey of life.

In essence, the dance between emotion and logic is the essence of being human. It is not about choosing one over the other, but understanding and valuing their intricate balance. By embracing both, we can lead lives that are not only successful in conventional terms but also deeply fulfilling and meaningful.

Success Factors: When EQ Matters More

As we delve deeper into the realms of human potential, the tug-of-war between EQ (Emotional Intelligence) and IQ (Intelligence Quotient) becomes more nuanced. Historically, IQ was the gold standard in predicting academic and, by extension, professional success. Cognitive prowess, as measured by IQ tests, was the beacon that guided many educational and occupational decisions. However, as our understanding of human dynamics, team synergy, and leadership qualities evolved, the spotlight has, in many contexts, shifted towards EQ.

One might argue that in a highly specialized profession, like quantum physics or advanced mathematics, IQ takes precedence. And while that might be true to an extent, even in such fields, collaboration, communication, and leadership play pivotal roles. These are arenas where EQ becomes indispensable.

Imagine a genius mathematician who comes up with groundbreaking theories but struggles to explain them to peers, fails to collaborate on research projects, or cannot mentor students effectively due to lack of empathy or understanding. The mathematician's genius, in the absence of emotional intelligence, remains isolated and, to a large extent, unrealized in its potential impact.

Several studies have demonstrated situations where EQ outshines IQ as a predictor of success:

1. **Leadership and Management:** Leading teams is not just about strategic decision-making but also understanding team dynamics, motivating team members, managing conflicts, and ensuring a cohesive, positive work environment. Leaders with high EQ

can read the emotional undercurrents of a situation and navigate them adeptly, ensuring not just productivity but also employee well-being.

2. **Sales and Customer Relations:** Being able to understand a customer's needs, concerns, and emotional drivers can often be the difference between making a sale or losing a client. The ability to empathize, connect, and build trust is central to client-facing roles.

3. **Negotiations:** Be it business deals, diplomatic negotiations, or even daily interactions, the ability to gauge the emotional stakes, understand unspoken concerns, and build rapport can determine the success of the negotiation.

4. **Mental Health and Well-being:** In personal spheres, high EQ individuals tend to have better mental health. They can recognize their emotional states, process their feelings, seek support when needed, and employ coping mechanisms more effectively. This emotional agility ensures resilience in the face of life's challenges.

5. **Teaching and Mentoring:** Effective education is not just about transmitting information but also inspiring, understanding individual student needs, and fostering a positive learning environment. Teachers with a high degree of emotional intelligence can create more impactful learning experiences.

In the bigger picture, IQ provides the tools – the analytical abilities, the cognitive skills, and the knowledge base. EQ, on the other hand, determines how effectively these tools are employed. It's the bridge between having a skill and effectively using it in the complex, multifaceted real world.

In today's interconnected global society, where teamwork, communication, and interpersonal dynamics are integral to both professional and personal spheres, EQ often emerges as the more significant success factor. It equips individuals to navigate the intricate web of human interactions, making the journey not just successful but also enriching.

In the intricate tapestry of human potential, it becomes evident that the role of Emotional Intelligence (EQ) extends far beyond just interpersonal interactions. It's woven deeply into the very fabric of our daily endeavors, aspirations, and long-term achievements.

While traditionally, intelligence as quantified by IQ was revered as the quintessential mark of a person's capabilities, the modern era, with its multifaceted challenges and layered interactions, demands a broader perspective. In this context, the significance of EQ emerges more pronouncedly.

In the realm of corporate leadership, for instance, the visionaries and leaders who leave a lasting impact often exhibit an uncanny ability to understand, empathize, and connect with a range of stakeholders - from employees and partners to customers and competitors. They innately grasp that the foundation of successful leadership isn't just strategic acumen but also the capability to foster trust, inspire loyalty, and cultivate an environment of mutual respect and understanding. These seemingly intangible qualities can be the difference between a company that merely survives and one that thrives, innovates, and leads its industry.

Moreover, in our increasingly globalized world, professionals traverse cultural, linguistic, and social boundaries regularly. Here, cognitive intelligence might assist in understanding market dynamics or technological nuances, but it's emotional intelligence that aids in navigating the subtle cultural sensitivities, understanding unspoken norms, and building genuine cross-cultural rapport. In such diverse settings, EQ becomes the linchpin, ensuring seamless interactions, fostering collaborations, and facilitating the exchange of ideas and values across borders.

Delving into the world of healthcare provides yet another testament to the power of EQ. Physicians, nurses, and healthcare professionals often find themselves at the intersection of science and humanity. While their technical expertise, grounded in years of rigorous training, is invaluable, it's their emotional intelligence that often dictates the quality of patient care. Being able to empathize with a patient's fears, communicate with compassion, and offer comfort in moments of vulnerability can be as healing as any medicine. In this sacred space, EQ stands shoulder to shoulder with medical knowledge, both indispensable.

Similarly, in academia, while subject-matter expertise is crucial, the most revered educators often possess a heightened sense of emotional intelligence. They can intuitively gauge a student's emotional state, tailor their teaching approach to resonate with diverse learners, and inspire not just academic excellence but also personal growth and self-awareness. The ripple effects of such emotionally attuned educators shape not just the trajectory of individual students but also the very ethos of institutions.

On a more personal front, emotional intelligence acts as an anchor in the tumultuous seas of relationships, be they familial, platonic, or romantic. In moments of conflict, it's often EQ that steers the ship, ensuring that disagreements don't escalate into irreversible rifts. In moments of joy, it amplifies the shared happiness, forging deeper bonds. In essence, EQ becomes the silent guardian, the unsung hero, nurturing relationships and ensuring their longevity.

In reflecting upon these myriad scenarios, one realization emerges with striking clarity: While IQ equips individuals with the tools to navigate the world's complexities, it's EQ that determines how gracefully and effectively they dance through its challenges. As the narrative of human progress continues to unfold, it becomes increasingly evident that the harmony between emotional and cognitive intelligence will be instrumental in scripting the most triumphant chapters.

Chapter 4: Emotional Intelligence in Relationships

Relationships stand as the central thread that binds our experiences, shaping our joys, sorrows, learnings, and memories. Whether they are fleeting or enduring, relationships are the mirrors reflecting our emotional depths and vulnerabilities. And in these complex relational dynamics, emotional intelligence, or EQ, emerges as a potent tool, allowing us to navigate the waters with grace, understanding, and depth.

Building intimate connections requires more than just shared interests or physical attraction. It necessitates a profound understanding of one's own emotions and an empathetic comprehension of the emotions of others. Imagine two individuals as two distinct universes. Each carries its own set of stars, planets, and mysteries. For these universes to harmoniously align, there needs to be a mutual resonance, an understanding of each other's orbits and gravities. This is where EQ plays its pivotal role.

Every individual comes with a past, laden with memories, traumas, joys, and lessons. While cognitive intelligence might aid in comprehending the facts of a person's history, it's emotional intelligence that allows us to feel the weight of their experiences, to empathize with their joys and pains, and to understand the nuances that lie beneath spoken words. When two people come together, whether in friendship, love, or any other form of relationship, they bring with them their emotional landscapes. These landscapes, shaped by past experiences, beliefs, cultural backgrounds, and personal narratives, often contain undulating terrains. Navigating these requires not just love or affection but also a heightened sense of emotional awareness.

Furthermore, emotional boundaries in relationships act as essential safeguards. They delineate where one individual ends and another begins. Respecting these boundaries signifies an understanding and acknowledgment of individual autonomy and personal space. Overstepping or ignoring these boundaries can lead to feelings of encroachment or violation, even if unintended. It's here that EQ aids individuals in recognizing, setting, and respecting these emotional perimeters.

Yet, as we delve deeper into relationships, we encounter the realm of emotional vulnerability. It's a space where our deepest fears, aspirations, insecurities, and dreams lay bare. While it's a space of immense emotional intimacy, it's also fraught with potential risks.

Being emotionally intelligent means understanding when to be vulnerable, recognizing the safe spaces where one's innermost feelings can be shared without the fear of judgment or betrayal.

In the grand tapestry of human existence, relationships, with all their complexities, beauties, and challenges, form the vibrant threads that add color, depth, and meaning. Emotional intelligence doesn't just enhance the quality of these relationships; it amplifies their essence, turning them from mere interactions into profound connections that enrich our lives in unimaginable ways.

Building Intimate Connections

Delving into the heart of relationships, one can't help but recognize that intimate connections form the bedrock of lasting bonds. These aren't merely connections defined by physical closeness, but by the profound intertwining of emotions, aspirations, vulnerabilities, and shared experiences. Building such connections is an art, enriched and facilitated by emotional intelligence.

At the genesis of every intimate relationship, there's often a mutual curiosity. This curiosity extends beyond knowing the mundane details of each other's lives. It seeks to understand the 'why' behind a person's beliefs, the stories that shaped their values, and the experiences that molded their personalities. Emotional intelligence guides this curiosity, ensuring it remains respectful, non-intrusive, and genuine.

Emotionally intelligent individuals often possess an innate ability to create a space of trust. This trust serves as the foundation for vulnerability, allowing individuals to share their fears, dreams, past scars, and future aspirations without fear of judgment. In doing so, they aren't just sharing information; they're opening up their emotional core, seeking resonance and mutual understanding.

However, building intimacy isn't a one-time event. It's a continuous process of mutual discovery, of understanding the evolving emotional landscapes of each other. As individuals grow, change, and evolve, their emotional needs, boundaries, and expressions shift. Recognizing these shifts, adapting to them, and providing the needed emotional support signifies a deep-rooted intimate connection.

The magic of such connections lies in their transformative power. They have the capability to heal past wounds, to provide a sense of belonging, and to inspire personal growth. In an intimate relationship, joys are magnified, and sorrows are shared, making life's journey more fulfilling and enriched.

Yet, it's essential to note that building intimate connections requires effort, patience, and understanding. Emotional intelligence provides the compass, guiding individuals through the complexities, ensuring that the connections remain genuine, respectful, and mutually nurturing. In essence, emotionally intelligent individuals don't just seek intimacy; they cultivate it, cherish it, and nurture it, turning fleeting connections into lasting bonds.

Real-life examples can provide a clearer understanding of concepts. Let's look at some scenarios that exemplify the role of emotional intelligence in building intimate connections:

1. Emily and Aiden's Reconnection: Emily and Aiden, former high school friends, reconnected during a reunion. While both had changed significantly over the years, their conversation flowed naturally. Emily had been through a challenging divorce, while Aiden had been exploring spiritual healing after the loss of a parent. Instead of sticking to surface-level pleasantries, they both displayed emotional intelligence by genuinely inquiring about each other's well-being. Aiden, noticing a hint of sadness in Emily's eyes when she mentioned her past, approached the topic with sensitivity. Emily, in turn, gave Aiden the space to share his spiritual journey without judgment. This emotionally intelligent exchange deepened their bond, turning a mere reunion encounter into a lasting friendship.

2. Raj's Understanding of Maria's Boundaries: Maria, an immigrant from Mexico, was dating Raj, who hailed from India. While both were deeply in love, they came from vastly different cultural backgrounds. During a dinner with Raj's family, Maria felt overwhelmed by the constant questions about her family and upbringing. Raj, sensing her discomfort, gently steered the conversation towards a more neutral topic. Later, he discussed the situation with Maria, ensuring he understood her boundaries. His ability to perceive and respect her emotional needs strengthened their relationship.

3. Sarah's Support for Leo's Dream: Leo always dreamt of starting a community theater but held back due to financial constraints and fear of failure. Sarah, his partner, recognized this unspoken dream of his. Using her emotional intelligence, she approached the topic, providing Leo with not just encouragement but also a safe space to voice his fears and apprehensions. Together, they brainstormed ideas, and Sarah's understanding and support eventually gave Leo the courage to pursue his dream.

4. Alex and Jordan's Weekly Check-ins: Alex and Jordan, roommates in college, established a weekly ritual. Every Sunday evening, they'd sit down for a 'check-in', discussing their highs and lows of the week. This wasn't just about sharing events but emotions, challenges, and personal growth moments. Their emotional intelligence shone through in these interactions, where they listened without judgment and offered support or advice only when asked. This ritual not only deepened their friendship but also provided them both with a trusted confidante.

These examples underline the fact that emotional intelligence isn't just about understanding one's emotions but also about recognizing and respecting the emotional currents in others. It's this mutual resonance that fosters intimate connections, turning relationships into rich tapestries of shared experiences and mutual growth.

Emotional Boundaries in Relationships

In the world of emotions, boundaries act as invisible lines that safeguard our emotional well-being. They represent our personal limits and are as essential as physical boundaries. While the walls of our homes protect us from external elements, emotional boundaries protect our internal world from potential emotional harm.

Each individual has their own unique set of emotional boundaries, shaped by personal experiences, upbringing, culture, and innate temperament. These boundaries define what is emotionally permissible and what isn't. For instance, while one person might be comfortable discussing their past traumas with a close friend, another might find such discussions deeply unsettling, even with someone they trust.

In relationships, respecting these boundaries is crucial. It's not uncommon for individuals, in their zeal to become close, to unintentionally overstep or ignore these emotional lines. Such actions, even if well-intentioned, can lead to feelings of discomfort, violation, or distress. For example, pressing someone to open up about a painful experience before they're ready can lead to them feeling pressured or unsafe.

The challenge here lies in identifying and communicating these boundaries. Not everyone is consciously aware of their own limits, and even fewer can articulate them effectively. Emotional intelligence plays a pivotal role in this. An emotionally intelligent individual is not only attuned to their own boundaries but can also perceive the unspoken boundaries of others. They can sense when a topic is causing discomfort or when a shared secret might be too heavy to carry for someone else.

Moreover, emotionally intelligent individuals know that emotional boundaries can evolve. A trauma survivor might initially be reluctant to share their experience, but with time, healing, and trust, they might decide to open up. Recognizing this dynamic nature and being patient is essential.

Another aspect to consider is the societal pressure to constantly share and bare our lives, especially in the age of social media. With people regularly sharing personal moments, achievements, and even grief online, the lines of what's private and what's public are constantly blurred. Here, setting firm emotional boundaries becomes even more critical to ensure one doesn't feel overwhelmed or exposed.

In essence, understanding and respecting emotional boundaries is about cherishing the sanctity of individual experiences. It's about acknowledging that while sharing is a path to closeness, true intimacy is achieved when both individuals feel safe, respected, and understood. Emotionally intelligent individuals don't just respect boundaries; they celebrate them as markers of individuality and personal resilience.

Emotional boundaries, at their core, aren't just protective barriers; they're reflective of our deepest values, beliefs, traumas, and triumphs. Each boundary, whether rigid or flexible, speaks of a history — of lessons learned, battles fought, trust broken, and love nurtured.

Consider the concept of trust. Trust is not just about believing someone will keep their word or act with integrity; it's also about believing they'll respect where we choose to draw our emotional lines. Each time a boundary is respected, trust deepens; each time it's crossed, trust erodes, often taking with it a piece of our emotional security.

In many traditional cultures, for instance, discussing personal hardships outside of the family is frowned upon. The emotional boundary here is defined by cultural norms. For someone from such a background, opening up about personal challenges to an outsider might feel like a betrayal of cultural values. An emotionally intelligent individual recognizes this and doesn't push for disclosure, understanding that emotional boundaries are sometimes tied to larger societal constructs.

Then there's the realm of personal traumas. For survivors of trauma, emotional boundaries often serve as crucial defense mechanisms. They are not just lines in the sand but fortresses built to guard against reliving traumatic experiences. Pressing a trauma survivor to share before they're ready isn't just a breach of trust; it's potentially retraumatizing. The emotionally intelligent approach here is to give space, to offer a listening ear without any obligation to fill the silence.

But it's not just about traumas or cultural values. Even in everyday relationships, emotional boundaries play a role. Think of a person who values their solitude, who finds rejuvenation in moments of quiet reflection. Their boundary might involve needing time alone after a long day. An emotionally intelligent partner or friend recognizes this not as rejection but as an essential self-care ritual.

Understanding emotional boundaries is also about recognizing that they can be fluid. Just as rivers change their course over time, our emotional boundaries can shift based on new experiences, healing, or personal growth. The boundary that seemed essential five years ago might seem irrelevant today. Or, a boundary that never existed before might suddenly become crucial due to a new life experience.

In delving deeper into the realm of emotional boundaries, one realizes that these aren't mere walls; they're windows into our soul's deepest corridors. They hint at our vulnerabilities and strengths, our fears and hopes. Respecting them isn't just about avoiding conflict; it's about honoring the intricate tapestry of experiences that make us uniquely human. The beauty of emotional intelligence lies in its ability to recognize these boundaries as sacred, to tread gently, and to honor the profound stories they silently narrate.

The Dynamics of Emotional Vulnerability

Emotional vulnerability, often misunderstood as a sign of weakness, is actually a testament to strength, courage, and authenticity. It's the willingness to open oneself up, to expose one's genuine emotions, fears, hopes, and insecurities, even at the risk of being hurt or misunderstood. In the realm of relationships, embracing emotional vulnerability is essential for forging deep, authentic connections.

When we talk about emotional vulnerability, we're addressing the innate human desire to be seen, understood, and accepted for who we truly are. Yet, this desire often comes into conflict with another primal urge: the need for self-preservation. Many people, conditioned by past hurts or societal expectations, wear masks or build emotional walls to protect themselves. While these defenses might offer a semblance of safety, they often come at the cost of true intimacy.

In the context of romantic relationships, vulnerability is the bridge that transforms superficial interactions into profound bonds. Consider two people starting a new relationship. In the beginning, exchanges are often light, filled with pleasantries and shared interests. Yet, as they begin to share their fears, aspirations, past mistakes, and dreams, the relationship deepens. These moments of vulnerability, where they lay bare their souls, are what lead to an unshakeable bond.

But emotional vulnerability isn't exclusive to romantic relationships. Even in friendships, family ties, or professional settings, allowing oneself to be vulnerable can lead to richer, more meaningful interactions. Sharing a fear with a colleague, expressing uncertainty about a big decision to a friend, or confiding a long-held dream to a family member—each of these instances fosters connection and trust.

However, it's crucial to recognize that vulnerability isn't about indiscriminate oversharing or burdening others with our emotions. It's a conscious choice, governed by discernment and trust. Not every situation or relationship demands vulnerability. It's the wisdom of knowing when to open up and when to hold back that's key.

Yet, the question remains: Why is vulnerability so challenging? The answer often lies in our past. Negative experiences, betrayals, or the societal glorification of stoicism and "toughness" can condition individuals to perceive vulnerability as a liability. Many fear that showing their true selves will lead to rejection, ridicule, or judgment.

However, the paradox of emotional vulnerability is that while it exposes one to potential pain, it's also the pathway to profound love, connection, and understanding. In a world often characterized by facades and superficial interactions, vulnerability stands out as an act of brave authenticity.

Embracing emotional vulnerability requires self-awareness, self-compassion, and courage. It's about recognizing and challenging the fears and beliefs that hold us back. And, in relationships, it's about creating a safe space where both individuals can be their authentic selves, without the fear of judgment.

In essence, understanding the dynamics of emotional vulnerability is about honoring the depth and complexity of human emotions. It's about celebrating the courage it takes to be genuine and recognizing the profound connections such moments can foster.

Emotional vulnerability, in its deepest sense, is an exploration into the caverns of the human heart. It's a journey that invites us to confront our innermost feelings, those tucked away memories, and the hidden facets of our psyche that we often hesitate to bring to the light.

At the very core of vulnerability lies the profound idea of "exposure." To be vulnerable is to lay oneself bare, open to the elements, be it criticism, empathy, misunderstanding, or love. And this exposure isn't a mere external act; it is intensely internal, a soulful unveiling. To be emotionally vulnerable is to allow someone else—maybe even yourself—a glimpse into the sanctum of your feelings, beliefs, hopes, and fears.

One might ask, why is this so profoundly difficult for many? The complexities stem from our evolutionary need for protection. From time immemorial, humans have associated exposure with potential danger. In the physical realm, this made sense, as exposure could mean vulnerability to predators or enemies. As societies evolved, this physical vulnerability translated into emotional and psychological vulnerability. Our ancestors learned that showing fear, uncertainty, or any form of perceived "weakness" could lead to exploitation by others. Over time, these protective mechanisms became deeply ingrained, leading to the guarded emotional behavior we often observe today.

Furthermore, the intricacies of modern society have layered additional challenges. Many cultures emphasize virtues such as stoicism, resilience, and unwavering strength, often associating vulnerability with weakness or instability. From a young age, individuals are conditioned to "keep a stiff upper lip," "not to wear their heart on their sleeves," or "be strong." Over time, these societal constructs can calcify into internal barriers, making the act of opening up feel perilous.

Yet, for all its perceived dangers, emotional vulnerability holds the promise of unparalleled richness. Every time we allow ourselves to be vulnerable, we tap into our most authentic self. It's like peeling away the many layers that life, society, and our experiences have wrapped around our core. And in that core lies our raw, unfiltered essence, where emotions reside in their purest form.

When two people share this essence with each other, the connection is transcendental. It surpasses the boundaries of mere human interaction and ventures into the realm of soulful communion. Such connections are not just about understanding; they're about deep resonance. It's like two melodies harmonizing, creating a symphony that's greater than the sum of its parts.

However, the journey into vulnerability isn't always linear. It requires patience and repeated acts of courage. Each venture into vulnerability might not be met with understanding or empathy. There might be instances of pain, of feeling exposed, or of regret. But like a muscle, the more one exercises vulnerability, the stronger it becomes. And with strength comes the wisdom of discernment—knowing when to be vulnerable, with whom, and to what extent.

In diving deeper into the world of emotional vulnerability, one doesn't just explore emotions but the very essence of humanity. It's a realm where fears and hopes coalesce, where tears and laughter are two sides of the same coin, and where, in the act of baring one's soul, one truly finds oneself.

Chapter 5: Emotional Intelligence at Work

In the bustling world of corporate affairs, boardroom meetings, and organizational hierarchies, emotions often take a backseat. The professional realm has traditionally emphasized metrics, logic, and strategy, often at the expense of recognizing the emotional undercurrents that undeniably influence decisions, interactions, and outcomes. However, as research and experience have revealed, emotional intelligence (EI) plays a pivotal role in determining success at work, far beyond just hard skills or technical expertise.

When you think about workplaces, consider the myriad interactions that happen daily. From a manager providing feedback to an employee, to team members collaborating on a project, or even a salesperson pitching a product to a potential client—all these interactions are laden with emotions, even if they're not always overtly expressed. Recognizing, understanding, and managing these emotions can profoundly impact the quality of these interactions and, by extension, the overall productivity and success of an organization.

Emotional intelligence isn't just about being "nice" or avoiding conflict. It's about fostering environments where people feel valued, understood, and motivated. In workplaces that prioritize EI, employees often report higher levels of job satisfaction, greater commitment to their roles, and improved interpersonal dynamics. Moreover, leaders with high EI tend to be better at motivating their teams, navigating organizational changes, and making decisions that consider the holistic well-being of their employees and the company.

But how does emotional intelligence manifest in everyday work scenarios? Imagine a manager faced with a team member who's consistently underperforming. A manager without EI might immediately resort to reprimands or even consider termination without delving into the reasons behind the underperformance. In contrast, a manager with high EI might approach the situation by trying to understand the root causes. Perhaps the employee is facing personal challenges, or maybe there's a skills gap that needs addressing. By approaching the issue with empathy and understanding, the manager not only stands a better chance at resolving the problem but also fosters a culture of trust and open communication.

Innovation, often hailed as the lifeblood of modern businesses, also thrives in environments that promote emotional intelligence. Creativity often blossoms in spaces where individuals feel safe to express their ideas, take risks, and potentially fail without facing harsh judgment. By cultivating a culture of emotional safety and understanding, organizations pave the way for out-of-the-box thinking and groundbreaking innovations.

Furthermore, in a globalized world, businesses often involve interactions with diverse cultures, backgrounds, and belief systems. Here, emotional intelligence becomes crucial. Understanding and respecting cultural nuances, adapting communication styles, and navigating diverse teams—all these require a keen sense of emotional acumen.

In summary, while hard skills, technical expertise, and strategic thinking are undeniably vital in the professional realm, the role of emotional intelligence cannot be underestimated. In the chapters that follow, we will explore various facets of EI at work, from leadership dynamics to team collaboration, and from decision-making to managing organizational changes.

Leading with Empathy

In the intricate tapestry of leadership qualities, empathy stands out as a golden thread, often underestimated but of immense value. Empathy, in the context of leadership, goes beyond simply understanding others' feelings. It is the ability to step into someone else's shoes, to view situations from their perspective, and to make decisions that resonate with their emotions and needs.

The rise of empathetic leadership can be attributed to a growing understanding of the complexities and diversities of modern workforces. Today's teams are a blend of multiple generations, cultural backgrounds, and personal histories. With such diversity, a one-size-fits-all approach to leadership no longer suffices. Leaders are now expected to navigate this intricate mosaic with sensitivity and insight, ensuring that every team member feels valued, understood, and inspired.

Empathetic leadership is also about active listening. It's not just about hearing words but discerning the emotions, intentions, and underlying concerns behind those words. When team members feel genuinely listened to, it fosters trust and creates an environment where they feel safe to voice their opinions, concerns, and ideas. This open channel of communication can be invaluable, providing leaders with insights that might otherwise remain obscured.

Additionally, leading with empathy has a profound impact on conflict resolution. Workplace conflicts, whether between team members or between management and employees, are often fraught with emotions. An empathetic leader can recognize the emotional undertones of these conflicts and address them at their root, rather than merely focusing on surface-level disagreements. By doing so, they can find resolutions that are not only effective but also conducive to long-term harmony and mutual respect.

However, empathy doesn't mean foregoing decisiveness or compromising on organizational goals. It's about balancing the human element with the strategic imperatives of an organization. Empathetic leaders can make tough decisions when needed but do so with a keen awareness of their impact on individuals and teams.

Real-world examples of empathetic leadership can be seen in how some leaders respond to crises or challenges. For instance, during times of organizational change or downturns, empathetic leaders communicate with transparency, provide clear rationales for decisions, and offer support to those affected. Their approach is not driven solely by bottom-line considerations but by a genuine concern for the well-being and future of their employees.

In a rapidly changing corporate landscape, where agility, innovation, and collaboration are prized, empathy emerges as a cornerstone of effective leadership. It's the bridge that connects leaders to their teams, fostering mutual respect, trust, and a shared sense of purpose. As we venture further into this chapter, we'll delve deeper into the nuances of empathetic leadership, its challenges, and its undeniable rewards.

Team Dynamics and Collective EQ

Teams, like individuals, have emotional lives. The collective mood, sentiments, and reactions within a team give rise to what can be referred to as the team's 'Emotional Quotient' or 'Collective EQ'. It represents how emotionally intelligent a team is as a unified entity, not just the sum of individual members' emotional capabilities.

In today's collaborative work culture, much of the organization's success depends on the performance of its teams. Whether it's a small project team, a department, or a cross-functional task force, the emotional dynamics within these groups significantly influence their productivity, creativity, and overall effectiveness.

The essence of collective EQ lies in how team members interact with each other. It's about the quality of interpersonal relationships, the level of trust, and the extent to which members feel safe to express their ideas and emotions. A team with a high collective EQ will exhibit effective communication, mutual respect, and a shared understanding of goals and values. They are more adept at navigating conflicts, are resilient in the face of challenges, and often display a strong sense of camaraderie.

However, achieving a high collective EQ isn't a given. It requires concerted effort, especially from team leaders. One of the critical factors is fostering an environment where open communication is encouraged. Team members should feel confident in expressing their viewpoints without fear of retribution or dismissal. This openness is particularly vital when addressing concerns, brainstorming ideas, or navigating disagreements.

Moreover, recognizing and celebrating the unique strengths and contributions of each team member can enhance the collective EQ. When individuals feel valued and acknowledged, it boosts their morale and encourages them to contribute more actively, strengthening the team's cohesion.

Another significant aspect is the acknowledgment and management of the emotional undercurrents within the team. Every team goes through highs and lows, periods of enthusiasm, and moments of frustration. Being attuned to these emotional shifts and addressing them proactively can prevent minor issues from snowballing into major conflicts.

Empathy, again, plays a pivotal role here. Teams where members display empathy towards each other tend to be more harmonious. They are better equipped to understand diverse perspectives, accommodate different working styles, and offer support during challenging times.

Effective teams also invest time in team-building activities. These don't necessarily have to be the typical corporate retreats or workshops. Even simple gestures like regular team lunches, celebrating birthdays, or acknowledging personal milestones can help in building bonds and elevating the team's collective EQ.

In essence, collective EQ is not just a desirable quality but a crucial one in today's collaborative and rapidly changing work environment. As teams become the fundamental units driving organizational success, their emotional intelligence, unity, and resilience will determine the heights they can achieve. As we continue in this chapter, we will explore the intricacies of nurturing collective EQ and the role of leadership in steering teams towards emotional maturity and excellence.

Emotional Intelligence in Decision Making

Decisions, large or small, are a constant in our lives, especially in professional settings. But what many might not realize is that our emotions deeply influence these decisions. Emotional intelligence, when integrated into the decision-making process, offers a balanced and holistic approach that can lead to better outcomes.

Every decision involves a blend of cognition and emotion. Logic provides the structure, the pros and cons, and the objective assessment. Emotions, on the other hand, give a personal touch, reflecting our values, desires, and fears. Both these aspects are crucial. Relying solely on logic might lead to decisions that seem perfect on paper but lack a human touch or adaptability. Conversely, being swayed entirely by emotions can result in impulsive or shortsighted choices.

People with high emotional intelligence have the ability to recognize their own emotional biases and the emotions of others. They can discern if they're feeling particularly optimistic or pessimistic and understand how that might color their judgment. For example, a manager might feel overly positive after a string of successful projects and might be inclined to take on a high-risk project without thoroughly analyzing its feasibility. Recognizing this emotional bias allows the manager to take a step back and re-evaluate.

Moreover, emotionally intelligent individuals also understand the emotions of stakeholders involved in or affected by the decision. They can anticipate reactions, address concerns, and ensure the decision aligns with broader team or organizational values.

Another essential aspect is the ability to manage the stress and anxiety that often accompany significant decisions. Indecision, fear of making the wrong choice, or the pressure from external sources can be paralyzing. Those adept in emotional intelligence can navigate these emotional turbulences, find clarity amidst the chaos, and move forward confidently.

Furthermore, emotionally intelligent decision-making also involves considering the emotional consequences of a decision. How will it affect the morale of the team? Will it lead to increased stress or potential conflicts? By anticipating these emotional outcomes, leaders can prepare, communicate effectively, and implement decisions in a way that minimizes negative emotional fallout.

Collaborative decision-making, another facet often seen in modern organizations, benefits greatly from emotional intelligence. In scenarios where multiple stakeholders are involved, the ability to understand, empathize, and communicate effectively becomes even more critical. Emotionally intelligent leaders can foster an environment where diverse viewpoints are heard, emotional undercurrents are recognized, and decisions are made that garner collective buy-in.

In essence, the realm of decision-making is vast and complex, influenced by an interplay of rational analysis and emotional undertones. By harnessing the power of emotional intelligence, individuals and organizations can make choices that are not only effective but also resonate with the heart and soul of the people they affect. As we delve further into this chapter, we'll explore real-life examples and scenarios where emotional intelligence made the difference between a good decision and a great one.

Emotions and decisions are intricately linked, often in ways we might not consciously acknowledge. To truly understand the depth of this relationship, we can look into the realms of neuroscience, behavioral psychology, and real-world scenarios that shed light on the profound impact of emotions on our choices.

At a neurological level, the brain doesn't treat emotional and rational processes as entirely separate. They are interconnected, with pathways linking the amygdala (responsible for emotions) and the prefrontal cortex (involved in cognitive processing). When faced with a decision, our brain doesn't merely weigh the logical pros and cons but also factors in emotional responses, past experiences, and even learned biases.

Consider, for instance, a scenario in which an executive has to decide between two potential hires. Both candidates have similar qualifications and experience. While one interview went smoothly with no hitches, the other was interrupted multiple times due to technical issues. On a purely logical level, these interruptions shouldn't matter. But the executive, influenced by the frustration and annoyance felt during the interrupted interview, might subconsciously favor the candidate from the smoother interaction. This bias, though subtle, is a direct consequence of the emotional experience.

Furthermore, emotions act as markers in our memory. Experiences accompanied by strong emotions, be it joy, fear, or anger, tend to be more vividly remembered. This emotional memory plays a silent role in our decisions. For example, an entrepreneur who previously faced a significant loss in a venture might hesitate to invest in a similar opportunity, even if logically, it looks promising. The emotional scar from the past failure serves as a deterrent, making the entrepreneur more risk-averse.

Emotional intelligence, in such scenarios, can be a game-changer. It equips individuals with the skills to recognize these emotional markers and biases. By being aware, one can choose to either factor them in the decision (if relevant) or consciously set them aside to avoid undue influence.

Behavioral psychology further supports this perspective. Studies have shown that people tend to make decisions that minimize emotional discomfort, even if it's not the most logical choice. The classic experiment by Tversky and Kahneman on loss aversion highlighted that people are more driven to avoid losses than to achieve gains, even if the net outcome is the same. This innate emotional response to potential loss can influence a myriad of decisions, from financial investments to personal relationships.

But it's not all about curtailing the influence of emotions. In many scenarios, emotions provide valuable insights. A gut feeling or intuition, often perceived as an emotional response, can be a culmination of subconscious observations and experiences signaling a particular decision. Emotionally intelligent individuals can discern when to trust these instincts and when to subject them to further scrutiny.

In summary, the deep dive into the relationship between emotions and decisions unveils a rich tapestry of influences. Emotional intelligence doesn't advocate for removing emotions from the decision-making equation but rather encourages a balanced, aware, and nuanced approach, where both logic and emotions work hand in hand to lead to choices that are both rational and resonate with our deeper human values and experiences.

Chapter 6: Challenges to Emotional Intelligence

In a rapidly evolving world, where technology, societal shifts, and global events are constantly reshaping our environments, emotional intelligence remains an essential skill. However, even as its importance grows, several modern challenges threaten to impede our emotional understanding and expression. This chapter delves into the obstacles and factors that can diminish or distort our emotional intelligence and how we can navigate these challenges to maintain genuine emotional connectivity with ourselves and others.

Our digital age, characterized by the ubiquity of screens, has redefined the ways we communicate and connect. While technology has bridged geographical divides, enabling instant communication across continents, it has, paradoxically, also contributed to emotional detachment. The sheer volume of interactions and information we process daily on digital platforms can lead to sensory and emotional overload, making genuine emotional engagement difficult.

Social media platforms, designed to connect people, often end up being a double-edged sword. On one hand, they offer a space for self-expression, networking, and access to a global audience. On the other, they can create an environment of constant comparison, where the curated lives of others can make individuals feel inadequate, leading to emotions of envy, loneliness, or low self-worth. The constant chase for validation through likes, shares, and comments can make emotions fleeting and superficial, contingent on external validation rather than internal self-awareness and reflection.

Moreover, the digital mode of communication, dominated by texts, emojis, and curated images, often lacks the richness of face-to-face interactions. The absence of vocal tones, facial expressions, and body language can lead to misinterpretations and miscommunications. Emojis, though designed to convey emotions, can hardly capture the depth and nuances of genuine feelings.

In addition to the digital landscape, our fast-paced lifestyles, characterized by packed schedules, multitasking, and the race against time, can leave little room for emotional reflection and mindfulness. The societal emphasis on productivity and efficiency, while essential in many contexts, can inadvertently sideline the importance of emotional health and understanding. Emotional reactions are often brushed aside as overreactions or weaknesses, discouraging genuine emotional expression.

Global events, whether it's a pandemic, political shifts, or environmental challenges, add another layer of emotional complexity. Collective anxieties, fears, and uncertainties can overshadow individual emotional processes, making it challenging to separate personal feelings from the broader societal mood.

Despite these challenges, it's essential to remember that our core emotional nature remains intact. Humans are inherently emotional beings, and while external factors can influence our emotional expression, they can't erase our emotional essence. The key lies in recognizing these challenges, understanding their impact, and actively seeking ways to cultivate and nurture our emotional intelligence amidst these external pressures.

In the subsequent sections of this chapter, we will explore each challenge in detail, offering insights, perspectives, and strategies to navigate the modern emotional landscape effectively. We will also delve into the tools, both digital and traditional, that can assist us in enhancing our emotional intelligence in these trying times.

Emotional Detachment in the Digital Era

The digital age has ushered in a plethora of advancements that have undeniably revolutionized the way we communicate, work, and live. However, this digital transformation also brings with it certain unintended side effects, chief among them being the phenomenon of emotional detachment.

The screens that dominate our lives — be it smartphones, computers, or tablets — promise connectivity, yet they often lead us to a state of emotional isolation. By enabling us to communicate without real-world interaction, these devices sometimes curtail the depth of our emotional exchanges. Each time we opt for a text instead of a call or a video chat instead of a face-to-face meeting, we miss out on the myriad of emotional cues that enrich human communication.

The immediate gratification and sensory stimulation provided by digital platforms are undeniable. Scrolling through a feed offers continuous novelty, engaging our attention in rapid succession. While this is exhilarating, it can also be emotionally numbing over time. The vast breadth of digital interactions can sacrifice depth. Instead of deeply engaging with a few posts or messages, users might find themselves skimming through hundreds, processing each only on a surface level. This superficiality, over time, can spill over into real-world interactions, making them equally cursory and lacking in emotional depth.

Online platforms, especially social media, have also redefined the concept of 'presence'. Even when physically present with loved ones, the allure of the digital world can pull us away, making us 'absent' in that very moment. This paradoxical state of being physically present but emotionally absent dilutes the quality of our relationships. The shared laughs, the silences, the spontaneous moments of affection — the very elements that enrich human relationships — get overshadowed by the constant digital interruptions.

Furthermore, the curated nature of online personas contributes to emotional detachment. The selective portrayal of life events, highlighting mostly the positives, creates a skewed reality. When individuals constantly view such 'perfect' lives, they might inadvertently suppress their genuine emotions, believing them to be out of place in this 'ideal' digital world. Over time, this suppression can lead to a disconnect between one's online persona and real self, making it challenging to identify and express genuine emotions.

Despite the challenges posed by the digital era, it's crucial to remember that technology is merely a tool. Its impact on our emotional well-being is largely determined by how we choose to use it. By being aware of the potential pitfalls and consciously prioritizing genuine human connections over digital distractions, we can harness the benefits of the digital age without compromising our emotional health. This balance is the key to ensuring that our digital lives enrich, rather than diminish, our emotional intelligence and well-being.

Social Media: A Double-Edged Sword

In today's interconnected society, social media stands out as one of the most influential forces. Platforms like Facebook, Instagram, Twitter, and TikTok have redefined not only the way we communicate but also the manner in which we perceive ourselves and the world around us. While the advantages of such platforms are manifold – fostering global connections, offering avenues for self-expression, and even catalyzing social movements – the ramifications on our emotional well-being can be profound and multifaceted.

The allure of social media lies in its promise of connection. For many, it provides a space where they can be heard, where they can share their joys, sorrows, aspirations, and thoughts. Yet, this same space, brimming with billions of voices, can sometimes make individuals feel even more isolated. The sheer scale of social media platforms can be overwhelming. Amidst the cacophony of posts, tweets, and stories, finding genuine emotional resonance can often seem like searching for a needle in a haystack.

Moreover, the curated nature of social media content, where individuals often present idealized versions of their lives, can create an environment of constant comparison. When continuously exposed to images of 'perfect' bodies, 'flawless' lifestyles, and 'enviable' achievements, it's easy to feel inadequate. This persistent feeling of 'not being enough' can erode self-worth and lead to feelings of discontentment, anxiety, and depression.

Another aspect of social media that impacts emotional intelligence is the reinforcement loop. Algorithms are designed to show users content that aligns with their beliefs, preferences, and past behaviors. While this ensures a customized user experience, it also creates echo chambers, limiting exposure to diverse perspectives and opinions. Such a filtered view can restrict emotional growth and understanding, making empathy towards differing viewpoints challenging.

The instantaneous nature of social media also affects emotional processing. In a world where reactions are sought and given in real-time, there's limited scope for reflection. An impulsive comment, a hasty like, or an instant share – actions that take mere seconds – can have lasting emotional implications, both for the initiator and the recipient. Such rapid emotional exchanges, devoid of deeper reflection, can contribute to volatility and misunderstandings.

Despite its challenges, social media, when used mindfully, can be a powerful tool for emotional enrichment. It can foster global communities of support, be a platform for artistic expression, and offer solace in moments of solitude. The key lies in recognizing its potential pitfalls and consciously navigating its vast expanse with emotional awareness and intent. By doing so, one can experience the connectivity it promises without succumbing to the emotional quagmires it can sometimes create.

In dissecting the multifaceted landscape of social media and its intricate relationship with our emotions, it becomes evident that its profound influence on modern life is a complex web of positive potential and latent pitfalls.

At its core, the very essence of social media thrives on validation. The system of likes, shares, and comments serves as an almost immediate feedback loop. For many, this feedback becomes a primary source of self-worth. A well-received post can boost confidence, elicit feelings of belonging, and create a sense of achievement. Conversely, a lack of engagement can induce feelings of rejection. The immediacy and scale of this validation mechanism mean that users can oscillate between emotional highs and lows several times a day. Over time, this emotional rollercoaster can affect the stability of one's self-esteem, making it contingent upon the unpredictable and often capricious reactions of the virtual audience.

The curated realities presented on social media platforms further complicate this emotional landscape. Behind every seemingly 'perfect' post lies a series of choices: which photo to share out of the dozens taken, which moment of the day to highlight, and which aspects of life to keep private. This curation, while natural, contributes to a phenomenon termed 'comparison fatigue'. As users continuously scroll through perfected snapshots of others' lives, they often subconsciously benchmark their own realities against these digital facades. This relentless comparison can be exhausting and can perpetuate feelings of inadequacy, even if intellectually, one understands that these portrayals are selective and polished.

The nature of discourse on social media platforms also merits attention. The limited character counts, the transient nature of stories, and the rapid pace of content dissemination don't always allow for nuanced discussions. Emotions, which are intricate by nature, get condensed into bite-sized, often oversimplified expressions. This truncation can sometimes rob emotional exchanges of their depth, leading to superficial interactions that barely scratch the surface of genuine human connection.

Moreover, the veil of anonymity or even physical distance that social media provides can sometimes embolden negative behaviors. Trolling, cyberbullying, and online harassment are dark aspects of the digital realm, where individuals, shielded by screens, sometimes unleash their basest impulses. Such actions can have profound emotional consequences, not just for the recipients but also for the perpetrators, perpetuating cycles of negativity and emotional turmoil.

Yet, amidst these challenges, the potential of social media to be a force of emotional good is undeniable. From global communities of shared interests and support groups for mental health to platforms for advocacy and awareness, social media holds the power to unite, uplift, and inspire. The challenge and opportunity for users lie in harnessing this potential while safeguarding their emotional well-being. It's a delicate balance, one that demands continuous introspection, awareness, and the courage to set boundaries when necessary.

Overcoming Emotional Overwhelm

As society progresses, there's a palpable sense of acceleration in every aspect of our lives. From the rapid pace of technological advancements to the whirlwind of information constantly available at our fingertips, there's an unrelenting influx of stimuli that demands our attention. This accelerated pace, while offering numerous advantages, also has an emotional cost. The ceaseless barrage of information, tasks, and decisions can lead to a state of emotional overwhelm.

Emotional overwhelm is a state where an individual feels swamped by their emotions, finding it challenging to process them effectively or to act rationally. It's akin to a cup filled to the brim, where any additional drop causes an overflow. This state can manifest due to various reasons – a sudden influx of unexpected news, a rapid succession of high-stress events, or even the cumulative effect of numerous small, unresolved emotional triggers.

In the context of modern life, the myriad sources of emotional overwhelm are numerous. Consider the daily digest of news, for instance. While being informed is essential, the relentless cycle of 24/7 news, often leaning towards the sensational and grim, can be emotionally taxing. Then there's the complexity of multitasking in the modern workplace and the juggling act of managing personal and professional commitments. Add to that the previously discussed impact of social media, and it becomes clear how easy it is to tip into a state of emotional inundation.

Overcoming this state is neither about denying emotions nor about striving for emotional detachment. It's about cultivating the ability to recognize the signs of impending overwhelm and developing strategies to navigate through it. Recognizing the early signs is crucial. It might manifest as a heightened state of anxiety, irritability, fatigue, or even a sense of numbness and disconnection.

Once recognized, several strategies can aid in navigating emotional overwhelm. Grounding techniques, which anchor an individual in the present moment, can be particularly effective. This might involve tactile activities like holding onto an object and focusing on its texture, engaging in deep breathing exercises, or even immersing oneself in nature. These activities act as circuit breakers, momentarily interrupting the emotional surge and offering a chance to recalibrate.

Another crucial strategy is the art of delegation and discernment. It involves recognizing one's limits and understanding that it's okay to ask for help or to prioritize tasks. This not only alleviates immediate stress but also ensures that one's emotional resources are directed towards truly significant concerns.

Furthermore, establishing a routine of regular emotional 'check-ins' can be beneficial. Just as one might take a break to stretch or have a glass of water, setting aside brief moments in the day to gauge one's emotional state can be invaluable. These check-ins, over time, can improve emotional resilience and offer clarity.

In an era marked by acceleration, mastering the art of managing emotional overwhelm becomes not just beneficial but vital. With conscious effort, it's entirely possible to navigate the complexities of modern life with emotional grace and resilience.

Chapter 7: Cultivating Emotional Intelligence

In the vast tapestry of human emotions, understanding and mastering one's own feelings can be a lifelong endeavor. Yet, it's an investment that promises unparalleled rewards. To navigate the intricate paths of relationships, personal growth, and self-fulfillment, cultivating emotional intelligence (EQ) is paramount. But how does one go about enhancing this invaluable skill?

Emotional intelligence isn't a static trait, cemented in childhood and immutable throughout life. It's dynamic, evolving with experiences, insights, and intentional efforts. Each person's EQ journey is unique, sculpted by their individual life story, challenges, aspirations, and strengths. However, there are common tools and practices that can universally aid in this journey.

The Role of Mindfulness Practices in Cultivating Emotional Intelligence

Mindfulness, as a concept, has roots that extend deep into ancient traditions, yet its relevance in the contemporary landscape is profoundly striking. Its role in cultivating emotional intelligence cannot be understated. It's a bridge, connecting our internal worlds to the external, fostering an awareness that is both introspective and expansive. By delving deeper into this relationship between mindfulness and emotional intelligence, we begin to uncover layers of understanding that reveal the intricate dance between perception, emotion, and cognition.

To truly understand the role of mindfulness in emotional intelligence, one must first grasp the essence of mindfulness itself. Mindfulness isn't merely about being present; it's an active engagement with the present. It invites individuals to experience moments with a depth that transcends mere acknowledgment. When you're mindful, you're not just seeing; you're observing. You're not just hearing; you're listening. This distinction, subtle as it may seem, has profound implications for emotional intelligence.

When applied to emotions, this heightened state of awareness enables individuals to not just identify feelings but to understand them. Why did a particular comment stir a pang of sadness? Why does a specific setting evoke feelings of unease? Mindfulness encourages this exploration, urging individuals to delve beneath the surface. It's a journey that often uncovers deeply ingrained beliefs, past traumas, or even societal conditioning that shapes emotional responses.

The true beauty of mindfulness, however, lies in its non-judgmental nature. In the realm of emotions, judgment often clouds understanding. One might chastise oneself for feeling jealous, anxious, or even overly excited. But mindfulness offers a different perspective, suggesting that there's no 'wrong' emotion. Instead of passing judgment, mindfulness teaches acceptance, fostering an environment where emotions, irrespective of their nature, can be understood and processed.

Moreover, the consistent practice of mindfulness enhances emotional granularity. This term, while not commonly discussed, is pivotal in the realm of emotional intelligence. Emotional granularity refers to the ability to differentiate between closely related emotions. For instance, recognizing whether one's feeling anxious, nervous, or apprehensive. While they may seem similar, each has nuances that dictate different responses. A mindful approach hones this ability to distinguish, leading to more effective emotional regulation.

The ripple effects of mindfulness extend beyond the self. By cultivating a deep, non-judgmental understanding of one's emotions, empathy towards others naturally flourishes. It becomes easier to resonate with others' feelings, to comprehend their emotional landscapes, and to offer genuine, heartfelt connections.

In essence, the role of mindfulness in cultivating emotional intelligence is multifaceted and profound. It's not just a tool but a philosophy, urging individuals to experience life with depth, compassion, and insight. Through mindfulness, the labyrinth of human emotions becomes less daunting and more intriguing, opening doors to understanding that enrich every facet of life.

Emotion-Focused Therapies

As the name suggests, emotion-focused therapies (EFTs) concentrate on emotions, specifically the transformation of emotion as a key element in therapeutic change. These therapies find their genesis in the belief that emotions can be a source of both dysfunction and healing. In the context of cultivating emotional intelligence, understanding and integrating the principles of EFT can offer a structured path to deepening one's emotional literacy.

Emotion-focused therapies argue that emotional responses are fundamentally adaptive and that they, in their pure form, can guide individuals to establish important needs and deal effectively with their environment. Yet, often due to past experiences, societal norms, or personal beliefs, these emotions can become suppressed, distorted, or over-amplified, leading to emotional disharmony. EFT seeks to provide a therapeutic environment where emotions can be safely explored, expressed, regulated, and transformed.

Within the framework of emotional intelligence, EFT holds significant promise. Firstly, it provides an avenue for individuals to explore their emotional reactions in a guided and supportive environment. Here, the narrative isn't about right or wrong emotions but about understanding, accepting, and potentially transforming emotional experiences.

For instance, someone who has always viewed anger as a "negative" emotion may, through EFT, come to understand the situations that trigger this anger, the underlying needs or values that are being threatened, and ways to constructively express and manage this emotion. This journey from raw emotion to constructive expression epitomizes the core of emotional intelligence: recognizing, understanding, and managing one's own emotions while also fostering empathy for others.

Emotion-focused therapies also emphasize the interconnectedness of emotions, cognition, and behavior. Emotional experiences aren't isolated events; they interact with our thoughts and subsequently influence our actions. By providing tools to dissect and understand these interactions, EFT aids in enhancing one's self-awareness, a cornerstone of emotional intelligence.

Lastly, EFT operates on the principle that emotional transformation is not only possible but also deeply healing. For individuals who may have spent years, if not decades, suppressing or avoiding certain emotions, this realization can be life-altering. By engaging with, rather than evading, one's emotional world, profound insights and growth can be achieved.

In the journey of cultivating emotional intelligence, emotion-focused therapies offer both a compass and a map. They guide individuals to delve deep into their emotional world, to embrace the full spectrum of their emotional experiences, and to emerge with a richer, more nuanced understanding of themselves and their relationships.

Emotion-Focused Therapies (EFTs) stand out in the vast landscape of psychotherapy as they are uniquely positioned to address the core of human experience: our emotional life. This emphasis on emotions, which are often the most immediate and poignant aspects of our existence, means that EFT dives directly into the heart of the matter. This therapeutic approach doesn't dance around the peripheries but tackles emotions head-on, unraveling their complexities and intricacies.

Every individual, irrespective of background or circumstance, carries an emotional tapestry woven through personal experiences. This tapestry, colorful and intricate, is made up of moments of joy, sorrow, anger, love, fear, and every shade of emotion in between. However, it's not uncommon for people to become estranged from certain threads of their emotional narrative. Societal expectations, past traumas, or learned behaviors can force individuals to cut away or bury specific emotional threads, believing them to be 'wrong' or 'undesirable.' EFT, in its essence, helps individuals to rediscover these lost or hidden threads and reintegrate them into the larger tapestry.

The beauty of Emotion-Focused Therapies lies in its therapeutic process. The journey typically starts with validation. Before diving into exploration or transformation, EFT recognizes and validates every emotion, emphasizing that every feeling has a reason and a right to exist. This validation serves as a balm to many, especially those who've felt emotionally marginalized or invalidated in the past.

After validation, the next step in EFT is exploration. This is where the therapy's transformative power begins to shine. Instead of merely acknowledging emotions, individuals are gently guided to dissect them, to delve deep into their origins, their triggers, and their patterns. For example, recurring feelings of resentment in a relationship might be traced back to childhood experiences of being overshadowed or not feeling heard. By pinpointing such origins, individuals can start to differentiate between past emotional baggage and present emotional reality.

Transformation, the final step in the EFT journey, is perhaps the most empowering. Once individuals understand and reconnect with their emotions, they are then equipped to transform them. This doesn't mean changing 'negative' emotions into 'positive' ones but rather reshaping emotional responses to be more adaptive and constructive. It's about channeling emotions, even intense or traditionally labeled 'negative' ones, in ways that are healing and growth-oriented.

The depth of Emotion-Focused Therapies is mirrored in its impact. As individuals rediscover and reintegrate their emotional selves, they often find that not only do they understand themselves better, but they also understand others. Empathy, compassion, and deep, meaningful connections become more attainable.

In conclusion, EFT isn't just a therapeutic approach; it's a journey of emotional rediscovery and reintegration. It calls to every individual, offering them a chance to reconnect with the most authentic parts of themselves and, in doing so, unlock the depths of emotional intelligence that reside within.

Daily Habits for Enhancing EQ

Our emotional intelligence (EQ) is not static; it can be cultivated, refined, and improved upon, much like a skill. One of the most practical ways of achieving growth in this area is through daily habits. Incorporating routines that emphasize self-awareness, regulation, and connection can have a transformative impact over time.

The most foundational aspect of emotional intelligence is self-awareness, and the practice of daily reflection can be instrumental in enhancing this. Setting aside a few quiet moments every day to introspect about emotional experiences can lead to profound insights. This could be done in the evening, reflecting on the day's events, emotions felt, and reactions given. Over time, this consistent reflection can lead to a clearer understanding of one's emotional patterns, triggers, and tendencies.

Another daily practice is the cultivation of mindfulness. While this term is often associated with meditation, it simply means being present in the moment. Mindfulness can be practiced during everyday activities, such as eating, walking, or even listening. By focusing entirely on the current activity and observing thoughts and emotions without judgment, individuals can become more attuned to their inner emotional landscape and the world around them.

Furthermore, journaling is an excellent tool for enhancing EQ. The act of writing down feelings and thoughts provides a safe space to process emotions. Over time, reviewing these journal entries can offer a bird's-eye view of emotional growth, patterns, and shifts.

Emotional regulation is another critical facet of EQ. Breathing exercises can be incorporated into daily routines to help in those moments when emotions run high. Just a few deep breaths can help lower anxiety and provide clarity. Similarly, practicing gratitude daily, perhaps by listing three things to be thankful for each morning or evening, can shift focus from what's lacking or overwhelming to what's abundant and positive in life.

Connection, both to oneself and others, is essential. Prioritizing meaningful conversations, even if brief, can be a game-changer. These don't always have to be deep or intense; just genuinely checking in with a loved one, a colleague, or even oneself can foster connection. Setting aside a few minutes each day for this can strengthen relationships and boost emotional understanding.

Lastly, continued education, like reading articles, books, or attending workshops focused on emotional intelligence, can further refine and expand understanding. Knowledge combined with daily practice can significantly elevate one's EQ journey.

By consciously incorporating these habits into daily life, individuals can lay down stepping stones toward heightened emotional intelligence. As days turn into weeks and weeks into months, the accumulated effects of these practices can lead to a richer emotional life, more profound connections, and an enhanced understanding of oneself and others.

Chapter 8: The Future of Emotional Intelligence

As the world hurtles forward, fueled by technological advancements and a myriad of sociocultural shifts, emotional intelligence (EQ) remains a potent, yet evolving, facet of the human experience. The importance of EQ in our past and present is undeniable, but what about its future? With every subsequent generation, the interplay between environment, upbringing, and technology redefines emotional landscapes, and it's pivotal to consider how these shifts will sculpt the role and significance of EQ in the days to come.

Emotions have been a constant across the evolutionary timeline of humanity, but the way we understand, express, and manage these emotions has undergone considerable transformation. The globalization of the modern age has brought diverse cultures into closer proximity than ever before. This intermingling has led to a richer tapestry of emotional understanding and expression. However, it has also brought to light the vast variations in emotional norms and values across different societies. As we venture into the future, the harmonization of these diverse emotional languages will become crucial.

Another profound shift lies in the realm of education. Traditional education systems have primarily focused on cognitive intelligence, often sidelining emotional development. However, as the benefits of EQ become more apparent and tangible, there's a palpable push towards integrating EQ education into mainstream curricula. Imagine a world where classrooms teach empathy with the same emphasis as algebra, where students learn the art of introspection alongside history lessons. Such an education model holds the promise of shaping emotionally attuned future leaders, thinkers, and innovators.

Yet, the most intriguing — and perhaps challenging — dimension of the future of EQ lies in the realm of technology. The digital age has already reshaped interpersonal dynamics, and as we stand on the cusp of the era of Artificial Intelligence (AI), the definition and domain of emotional intelligence are set to undergo unprecedented transformation.

Can machines ever truly understand or possess emotional intelligence? On the surface, it seems like an oxymoron. Emotions, with their organic, raw, and often irrational essence, stand in stark contrast to the logical, binary world of machines. Yet, advancements in AI have already shown capabilities that mimic emotional understanding. AI chatbots designed for therapy, robots capable of reading facial expressions to gauge mood, and algorithms predicting emotional responses are no longer the stuff of science fiction. They are our reality.

But while machines might mimic or recognize emotions, can they ever truly 'feel'? And as these AI entities become more embedded in our daily lives, how will they impact human EQ? Will our emotional growth be stunted by relying too heavily on AI companions and tools, or will they offer avenues to enhance and elevate our emotional landscapes?

In the convergence of technology and emotion, ethical questions also emerge. The responsibility of using and developing emotionally intelligent AI, the boundaries of privacy, and the potential psychological implications for individuals are topics that society will grapple with.

In conclusion, the future of emotional intelligence promises to be as complex and multifaceted as the emotion itself. While challenges lie ahead, so do immense opportunities for growth, understanding, and connection. As humanity moves forward, the compass of EQ, guiding us through interpersonal intricacies and technological mazes, will be more crucial than ever.

Machines and EQ: An Oxymoron?

The juxtaposition of machines — logical, predictable, and binary — with emotional intelligence — organic, fluid, and complex — at first glance appears paradoxical. But as technology relentlessly advances, intertwining ever more intimately with our lives, it begs the pressing question: Can machines ever truly possess or understand emotional intelligence? And if they can, what are the implications for human society?

The realm of artificial intelligence (AI) has made leaps that seemed unfathomable just decades ago. Machines can now recognize human faces, interpret vocal intonations, and even predict emotional responses based on data patterns. These capabilities have fueled the rise of emotionally-responsive robots, AI therapists, and customer service chatbots that can gauge and adapt to the user's emotional state. For industries, this is groundbreaking. It offers the potential for more personalized user experiences, more effective therapeutic tools, and more efficient service models.

Yet, the essence of emotional intelligence goes beyond mere recognition and response. It's rooted in understanding, empathy, and genuine connection. While a machine can be programmed to recognize a frown and respond with a comforting phrase, it does not 'feel' concern or empathy in the human sense. Its response is based on algorithms and pre-defined protocols, not genuine emotion.

This brings forth the philosophical debate about the nature of consciousness and emotion. Can emotion ever be genuinely replicated, or is it an inherently human experience, bound intrinsically to our biology and consciousness? While technology can simulate and emulate, there's a depth to human emotion that, many argue, cannot be truly mirrored by machines.

However, this distinction between human emotional experience and machine-emulated emotionality becomes blurrier with the rise of neural networks and deep learning. These sophisticated AI models are designed to mimic the human brain's structure and functionality. As they 'learn' from vast amounts of data, their responses become less predictable and more organic, closely resembling human-like thought processes. But even with these advancements, the debate remains: Does this mimicry amount to genuine emotional intelligence or a sophisticated imitation?

Furthermore, as machines become more integrated into our emotional landscapes, there are potential societal ramifications. For instance, if an individual relies heavily on an AI companion for emotional support, does it diminish their capacity for human connection? Or does it provide invaluable support, especially in scenarios where human interaction might be limited or detrimental?

The integration of machines into the world of emotional intelligence is a journey filled with potential, intrigue, and ethical dilemmas. As technology continues to progress, society will grapple with these questions, navigating the intricate dance between human emotion and machine intelligence. Whether viewed as a harmonious union or a challenging paradox, the relationship between machines and EQ will undeniably shape the trajectory of our future.

Anticipating the Next Wave in Emotional Evolution

Emotional intelligence has undergone significant evolution throughout human history, adapting and transforming in response to societal changes, technological advancements, and shifts in human understanding. As we look towards the future, it's imperative to anticipate the next wave of emotional evolution and the factors that will shape it.

The rapid pace of technological change in the 21st century brings about a series of emotional challenges and opportunities. For one, the very nature of human connection is evolving. With the rise of virtual realities, augmented realities, and immersive digital experiences, the lines between the tangible and intangible are becoming increasingly blurred.

In such a landscape, understanding and expressing emotions might take on new dimensions. People might soon find emotional connection and catharsis in virtual environments, seeking solace in digital realms or forging relationships with virtual entities.

Moreover, as global connectivity increases, so does exposure to a diverse range of cultures, beliefs, and emotional languages. This heightened global interconnection will necessitate an evolved form of emotional intelligence, one that is attuned to a broader spectrum of emotional expressions and norms. Recognizing and respecting emotional cues from a variety of cultural backgrounds will be vital. This globalized emotional intelligence will pave the way for more inclusive, understanding, and harmonious cross-cultural interactions.

Additionally, advancements in neuroscience and psychology are continually shedding light on the intricacies of the human emotional landscape. As we gain deeper insights into the workings of the human brain, emotions, once thought to be intangible, might become quantifiable, mappable entities. This scientific understanding can significantly influence how we teach, foster, and harness emotional intelligence. For instance, if we can pinpoint neural pathways responsible for empathy, can we then enhance or train these pathways more effectively?

However, with these advancements also come ethical considerations. If emotions can be mapped and potentially modified, where do we draw the line? The idea of 'engineering' emotional experiences or responses might become a contentious topic, challenging our notions of authenticity and free will.

Another potential driver for emotional evolution is the environmental crisis. As communities grapple with the implications of climate change, there's a collective emotional reckoning at play. The shared grief, anxiety, and determination spurred by environmental challenges can shape a new form of emotional bonding and understanding among global citizens. Emotional intelligence will play a pivotal role in mobilizing and uniting individuals towards collective action.

In essence, the next wave of emotional evolution is poised to be a multifaceted interplay of technology, science, global connectivity, and environmental consciousness. Preparing for this wave requires foresight, adaptability, and a deep commitment to understanding the ever-changing tapestry of human emotion.

Conclusion

Emotional intelligence, as explored throughout this book, is a rich, multifaceted domain deeply interwoven into the human experience. From its historical underpinnings to its role in shaping relationships, workplace dynamics, and our interaction with emerging technologies, EQ presents itself as a vital skill set for the modern world.

Reflecting on our journey, we began with a foundational understanding of what emotional intelligence entails. Through the chapters, it was clear that EQ is not merely about recognizing and labeling emotions but extends to how we manage our feelings, navigate social landscapes, and forge meaningful connections. This intricate dance between self-awareness, self-management, social awareness, and relationship management forms the four pillars of EQ, each holding its significance in the tapestry of human interactions.

The connection between EQ and IQ provided insights into how emotion and logic, seemingly opposing forces, actually work hand in hand to shape our responses and decision-making processes. While IQ provides the cognitive ability to process information, EQ ensures that this processing is aligned with our emotional landscape, guiding actions that resonate with our inner values and the environment around us.

Furthermore, the chapters on emotional intelligence in relationships and at work underscored the practical applications of EQ. We discovered how emotional attunement can strengthen intimate bonds, foster teamwork, and enhance leadership qualities. On the flip side, we also delved into the challenges that the digital age presents to emotional intelligence, exploring how over-reliance on technology might impede genuine emotional connections.

Our exploration took a futuristic turn as we dived into the world of machines and EQ. The intriguing prospect of AI possessing or emulating emotional intelligence led us to ethical dilemmas and philosophical musings about the very nature of emotions. Can they be replicated? Is there a genuine essence to human feelings that machines will never grasp? These questions, though unanswered, will undoubtedly shape the trajectory of technology and human interactions in the coming decades.

Lastly, anticipating the next wave in emotional evolution, we envisioned a future where EQ will have to adapt and transform in response to global challenges, technological advancements, and a deeper scientific understanding of emotions. Whether it's the rise of virtual realities, the intricacies of global emotional languages, or the shared emotional responses to global crises, the evolution of EQ will remain a testament to the adaptability and resilience of the human spirit.

In closing, the journey through emotional intelligence illuminates a fundamental truth: At the heart of our most profound decisions, interactions, and innovations lie our emotions. Mastering the art of understanding, expressing, and navigating these emotions is the key to leading a fulfilled, harmonious, and impactful life. As the writer James Baldwin beautifully put it, "The world is yours to shape, but first, the journey begins within." Embrace the voyage of emotional discovery, for it is within this realm that true mastery of the self and the world around us lies.

The study and understanding of emotional intelligence is an ongoing pursuit. Much like a river that continuously flows and reshapes its course, the realm of EQ is dynamic, influenced by our ever-evolving societal constructs, personal experiences, and the vast reservoir of human knowledge. Engaging with EQ is not a one-time endeavor but a lifelong journey of mastery.

In our lifetime, we undergo countless experiences, both joyous and challenging. Each of these moments offers an opportunity to engage with our emotional self. For instance, consider the experience of a young child heading to school for the first time. The mix of excitement, anxiety, curiosity, and maybe even a little fear is a whirlwind of emotions. As the child matures, they might experience their first heartbreak, the thrill of achieving a goal, or the grief of losing a loved one. Each of these experiences deepens their emotional reservoir, helping them understand and navigate feelings better.

The societal shifts we experience further mold our EQ journey. Consider the rise of digital communication in the last few decades. While the internet has brought the world closer, it also poses challenges to authentic emotional interactions. The emojis and GIFs we use in digital conversations are a testament to our continuous endeavor to convey emotions, even in the absence of face-to-face interactions. However, the nuances of tone, facial expressions, and body language are harder to capture, requiring us to refine and adapt our emotional understanding in this digital age.

Moreover, as we've touched upon earlier, the advancements in neuroscience, psychology, and even artificial intelligence have deep implications for EQ. As science unravels more about the brain's emotional centers, our methodologies for EQ training, therapies, and interventions might see significant shifts.

One might wonder, with such a vast and dynamic domain, can one ever truly master emotional intelligence? The truth lies in understanding that mastery is not a final destination but an ongoing process. The beauty of EQ lies in its endless depth. There's always more to learn, understand, and implement. The pursuit of EQ mastery, thus, is about continuous growth, reflection, and adaptation.

This journey is not without its challenges. There will be moments of emotional overwhelm, misjudgments, and perhaps even regret. However, each stumble is a lesson, a stepping stone towards a deeper emotional connection with oneself and the world around.

It's essential to understand that emotional intelligence, in its core, is about harmony. It's about aligning our inner emotional world with the external environment, creating a symphony of interactions, decisions, and experiences that resonate with authenticity and depth.

So, as you continue your journey in life, cherish the emotional landscapes you traverse. Engage with them, learn from them, and remember that the path to EQ mastery is a continuous, enriching voyage that adds depth and color to the tapestry of human existence.

Regards and Bonus

Dear Reader,

Firstly, a heartfelt thank you for investing your time and trust in "Emotional Intelligence 2.0." It's been a profound journey crafting this book, and I genuinely hope it has offered valuable insights and tools to enhance your emotional landscape.

Your feedback means the world to me and others who might be considering embarking on this journey with us. If you found value in these pages, I kindly ask you to take a few moments to leave an honest review on Amazon. Your insights not only help potential readers discern if this book is right for them but also guide me in understanding how to better serve readers like you in the future.

Exclusive Bonus for Our Readers:

As a token of my gratitude, I'm thrilled to offer you an exclusive bonus - the audiobook version of "Emotional Intelligence 2.0." Whether you're on the move, working out, or simply want to revisit the content in a new format, the audiobook is a fantastic companion.

To access your bonus, simply scan the QR code on the next page. It's that easy!

Your journey with emotional intelligence doesn't end with the last page of this book; in many ways, it's just beginning. And I'm honored to be a part of it.

Thank you once again, and here's to a life rich with emotional depth and understanding.

Made in United States
Troutdale, OR
11/03/2023

14273450R00044